WHY AM I STILL HERE?

TESTIMONIALS

"If you are in a season of waiting, or a season that requires you to have more trust, I would highly recommend picking up this book and asking God to speak to you through it. Thank you Amanda for your obedience in the wait. I cannot wait to see where God takes you." - *Michelle Apples, Founder of the Christian Singles Hub and Miss Apples Matchmaking*

"Why Am I Still Here? is a great book on diving into the issue of trust with God and others. I really recommend reading this book if you want to to dive deeper in your relationship and trust in God."- *Rachel Rasch, Blogger of the Olive Press Co.*

"I needed to be reminded that I wasn't alone in this season, that this season wasn't going to break me." "The length of my wait does not determine the fulfillment of my promise." These quotes sum it up for me. The book is easy to read and very relatable. The author gives practical advice on how to thrive in any season of waiting and gives the reader hope. - *LaToya Wilmot-Brown, Founder of LWB Creations and Toya Loren*

WHY AM I STILL HERE?

LEARNING TO TRUST GOD IN THE WAITING

AMANDA GUISEPPI

Copyright© 2022 Amanda Guiseppi

All rights reserved. No portion of this book may be reproduced, stored in a retrieval system, or transmitted in any form or by any means- electronic, mechanical, photocopy, recording- except for brief quotations in critical reviews or articles, without the prior written permission of the publisher.

ISED #: 1190320
ISBN: 978-1-7780749-0-5

The events in this book are my memories from my perspective.

Scripture quotations marked NLT are taken from the Holy Bible, New Living Translation, copyright © 1996, 2004, 2015 by Tyndale House Foundation. Used by permission of Tyndale House Publishers, Carol Stream, Illinois 60188. All rights reserved.

Scripture quotations marked TPT are from The Passion Translation®.
Copyright © 2017, 2018, 2020 by Passion & Fire Ministries, Inc. Used by permission. All rights reserved.

Scripture quotations marked NKJV are taken from The Holy Bible, New King James Version, Copyright © 1982 Thomas Nelson. Used by permission. All rights reserved.

Scripture quotations marked ESV are taken from The Holy Bible, English Standard Version® (ESV®), Copyright © 2001 by Crossway, a publishing ministry fo Good News Publishers. Used by permission. All rights reserved.

Scripture quotations marked NIV®are taken from The Holy Bible, New International Version®, Copyright © 1973, 1978, 1984, 2011 by Biblica, Inc.® Used by permission. All rights reserved worldwide.

Scripture quotations marked NIVUK are taken from The Holy Bible, New International Version® (Anglicised), NIV®, Copyright © 1979, 1984, 2011 by Biblica, Inc.® Used by permission. All rights reserved worldwide.

Scripture quotations marked (GNTD) are from the Good News Translation (US Version) in Today's English Version- Second Edition Copyright © 1992 by American Bible Society. Used by Permission.

Scripture quotations marked from the Common English Bible®, CEB® Copyright © 2010, 2011 by Common English Bible.™ Used by permission. All rights reserved worldwide.

Scripture quotations marked AMP are taken from The Amplified® Bible, Copyright © 2015 by the Lockman Foundation. Used by permission. All rights reserved.

Scripture quotations marked MSG are taken from The Message. Copyright © 1993, 1994, 1995, 1996, 2000, 2001, 2002. Used by permission of NavPress Publishing Group.

Front cover, book design and back cover created through Canva.

Printed by Sure Print & Design in Canada.

First printing edition 2022.

Amanda Guiseppi
103 1/2 Canada Street
Hamilton, ON, Canada
L8P 1P3

amandatheauthor.com

I dedicate this book to God who uses every situation in my life, including a global pandemic such as COVID-19, to help me grow. Without the lockdowns our country went through, I wouldn't have been able to write this book and thus find my journey to fully trust Him.

AUTHOR'S NOTE

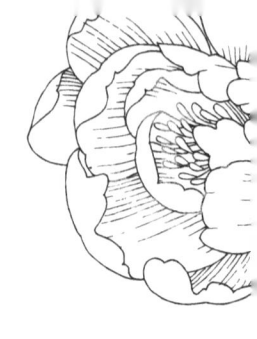

Please note that all biblical references and Scriptures used in this book reflect the author's experiences and in no way are meant to be reflected as theological impressions and interpretations of the Bible.

CONTENTS

Prologue	i
Introduction: Defining Trust	1
Chapter 1: Don't Doubt in the Light	12
Chapter 2: Trust is a Choice	24
Chapter 3: What It Means to Trust God	44
Chapter 4: Trust is a Heart Issue	70
Chapter 5: Trust is Active	85
Chapter 6: Waiting Well	107
Chapter 7: Keep Your Eyes Up!	138
Chapter 8: His Will, Not Mine	161
Chapter 9: Trusting God's Will	184
Chapter 10: God's Timing is Perfect	203
Chapter 11: God Always Comes Through	226
Conclusion	253

Bibliography
Resources
About the Author
My Previous Books
First Readers Club

PROLOGUE

Dear Reader,

This book is for those of you who have been waiting on your promise for years. Maybe it's a baby, a new job, breakthrough, restoration of a relationship, or that next season? If truly honest with yourself, you have given up at times and doubt that it will come to pass. This book is for those running the race but feel like you aren't going anywhere. This book is for the discouraged thinking, "Why am I still here?" "Why haven't things changed yet?" "Why haven't I received my promise?" It's for those of you who have lost hope. Or maybe you are hopeful, faithful and doing everything right, but you are still waiting. This book is also for you. This book is for those sinking their teeth into the promises of God and refusing to let go until they see it manifested in their life.

Join me as I share about the natural ups and downs and ebbs and flows of waiting and learning to trust God throughout it all. My waiting story started when I was a little girl. I have been waiting for my dreams to come true since I was 5 years old. Sure, over the years, I have learned to lay down those dreams and trade them in for the promises of God. However, over 30 years later, I am still waiting. So, to say that I know about waiting and trusting God is an understatement.

I am there with you if you are in the Land of Discouragement, on Doubt Avenue or on Fear Boulevard. I have been through it all, but I have learned how to trust God in the midst. Come on this journey with me and discover the secret to waiting well and trusting God throughout it all.

My prayer as you read this book is that you will not just see it as another book on your list of books to read. However, you would use the pages within to interact with my story and find your own journey to trusting God.

There are many ways to interact with this book:

Journal prompts: You will see journal prompts throughout the book. I want to encourage you to take some time and journal, whether it's within the book or you use your own journal.

Doodles: I have provided space for you to unleash your creative side and draw, doodle, paint, use markers, whatever you want. I find sometimes seeing something is more impactful than reading it.

Questions: I have provided questions throughout this book to allow you to think through how it relates to your own life. Take some time and answer them, pray through them and let God show you something new.

On this journey with you,
Amanda

INTRODUCTION

WHAT IS TRUST?

My hope with this book is to help you understand what trust is - genuine biblical trust, and what that looks like in your own life.

> *Trust is not a passive state of mind. It is a vigorous act of the soul by which we choose to lay hold on the promises of God and cling to them despite the adversity that at times seeks to overwhelm us.*- Jerry Bridges[i]

Trust is not passive; it is active. It is an active choice on our part to choose to "lay hold" of the promises of God despite what our circumstances tell us - despite the adversity we face in life. Jerry Bridges takes it one step further to say that trust is clinging to those promises.

How many of us know that when God speaks a promise to us, we don't usually see the manifestation of that promise right away? It takes time, and in that waiting time, difficulties may arise. Those difficulties come so that our character can be shaped and moulded. God doesn't want to bless us prematurely and have us not enjoy His blessing. The Bible states that He blesses us, and there is no sorrow added to it (Proverbs 10:22). He wants to bless us, but He also wants us to enjoy that blessing. In the meantime, He shapes and moulds our character through our circumstances.

Therefore, trust is saying that we will hold onto that blessing no matter what comes our way. No matter what test God wants to put us through or tribulation we face. Our confidence comes from God, our promise keeper. We know that he is not a man who should lie, the son of man who should change his mind (Numbers 23:19). So, what he says will come to pass.

That seems straightforward, but let's take it one step further. The word trust shows up in the Old Testament of the Bible 158 times. The Hebrew term for trust, the language of the Old Testament, is *batach*. It means "to lie extended on the ground" or "to throw one down upon his face."[ii]. So to trust someone in the Old Testament days was to be so comfortable and vulnerable around them that you let your guard down and allow them to see your back.

This type of trust was intimacy and vulnerability. It was letting someone into your life, your heart and your spirit. This type of trust takes intimacy. You need to know the other person. God desires this type of intimacy with us. He wants us to let our guards down when we are around him. He wants us to know that he is a safe harbour always (Psalm 91:2).

The mere thought of this type of trust sends my mind into a frenzy. I didn't trust well. I know what you're thinking, then why am I writing a book about trust? The answer is simple, I want to fully trust no matter what happens in my life. I want to be that person who trusts God so much that whatever comes my way, I can face it with confidence knowing that God has me. He has my best interest at heart. Not only do I want to trust God, but I want to learn to trust others.

Due to my past, I have learned a lot about how **not** to trust God. When I meet someone in my life, I begin to trust them over time, and then they break that trust. In the end, I am struggling to regain that trust in them I once had. This pattern has happened in my life several times, especially with those closest to me. I have yet to meet a person in my life that I explicitly trust. I had even struggled to trust God at times when my life didn't look the way I thought it would.

MY TESTIMONY

Trust
She expected, she hoped, and she assumed,
That she would be protected;
From the harsh and cold world.
Those who came before her,
Know the way.
They guide, they teach, and
They protect.
But not this time,

They took advantage,
Of an innocence;
Held so dear.
They forced and pushed.
Behind closed doors;
Under bed sheets;
In the dark;
They tore apart naivety,
Until there was nothing left,
But a shell.
She learned to hide;
She learned to numb the pain.
She closed down
The doors to her heart.
So that no one
Could come in.
Trust was ripped away;
Love was a distant memory.

I need to take you back to the beginning to understand my trust issues. Before the age of ten, I experienced fourteen acts of sexual molestation/assault by ten different people in my life. Three of these people were family members and close friends who were supposed to protect me.

I learned from a young age that adults took advantage of children; that's just what happened. I hid behind my pride and self-rejection so that no one would come close. I would love to say that it got better, but it only worsened. By high school, I fell into depression and began to have frequent panic attacks and suffered from anxiety and insomnia.

As someone who didn't love herself and loved others even less, I had nowhere to turn. I turned to drugs, alcohol and men to ease the pain inside me. You see, I didn't trust men, but I thought I could use them the way they used me. I had to have the power; I had to be in control. This season of my life left me feeling empty. I still suffered from panic attacks, anxiety and depression but now hated myself for what I did. This lifestyle wasn't me, and I knew it, but I didn't know how to stop it.

But then Jesus. At the end of 2009, a friend of mine invited me to church. I hadn't been to church in a long time, but something inside me thought maybe I should go. 2009 had been a bad year for me; I almost lost my job and ultimately lost my Work Visa.

That meant I would have had to go back home to Canada. I needed something positive in my life. Through this church, I took the Alpha Course, a course designed to explore the essentials of faith. At the end of this course, I decided to say yes to Jesus.

Jesus was on a rescue mission over 2000 years ago to save little old me, and you too! That just blew my mind. To know that there was someone out there that truly loved me for me - all of me. Someone willing to love me all the way back to wholeness. To see all of my flaws but decide to love me anyway. I couldn't understand it, and all I could do was embrace it.

WHY I WRITE ABOUT TRUST

God asked me to write about trust a couple of years ago when I was knee-deep in struggling to trust Him in my life. In a season where I felt stuck, I questioned everything in my life, and I couldn't wrap my mind around why I was where I was. The question "Why am I still here?" rang true in my head regularly. I knew where I wanted to go, but I grappled with why I wasn't there yet and discontentment in where I currently was. Nothing I wanted in life was present, and I blamed God.

One day during my prayer time, the Holy Spirit whispered into my heart that I would write a book on trust. The thing was that one of my dreams was to become a professional writer. This dream was birthed after writing my first book. However, my first book didn't do as well as I would have hoped, so I gave up on my dream of being an author. I remember thinking that there was no way I would write again. What was God thinking asking me to write about trust?

But like any good Christian girl, here I am, being obedient, writing about the one topic I struggled with. I know that God is trustworthy, but I wasn't sure how to find my way back to trusting Him after everything I had been through. Isn't that where God wants us? Struggling, but willing? Will you come with me on this journey of finding our way back from disappointments, hurt, deception, abuse, heartache and overcoming our past to embrace a new future of trusting God?

WHY DON'T WE TRUST?

So why don't we trust? Well, you could be like me and have experienced trauma at the hands of someone else that has caused you to be cautious about who you trust or if you trust at all? Or, perhaps, you find the idea of letting someone that close to you petrifying, so you choose not to trust. Whatever your reason is, I believe God wants to restore that to you. He created us for intimacy. He made us for love. Out of that intimacy naturally comes trust.

Let's look at Moses' story and his journey to trust God - from an unknown God to a God that he knew so intimately. Our story starts in the book of Exodus. Moses was born at a very trying time in Israelite history. King Ramses ruled over Egypt at the time. He was the next king after the one who led with Joseph. He had no previous knowledge about what Joseph had done for the country during the famine. He made a decree out of fear that the Israelites would outgrow them in number and rebel. When the Egyptian midwives would help an Israelite woman give birth, they would look out for the baby, and if it were a boy, they would have to kill it. Alternatively, if it were a girl, they would let her live (Exodus 1:16).

When Moses was born, his mother saw that he was special and hid him for three months (Exodus 2:2). When she could no longer hide him, she placed him in a basket and put it in the Nile River. The King of Egypt's daughter found the baby in the river and took him in as her own. She named him Moses because she lifted him out of the water. The word Moses sounds like the Hebrew word "*Mosheh*," which means "to draw out."[iii]. He ended up being raised in the palace while the King oppressed his people.

When Moses was older, he ended up re-settling in his people's land, the Israelites and got married (Exodus 3:21). At this time, his people were still enslaved and under great oppression. Then he encountered God. He had probably heard of Him in later years but never knew Him. God asked him to trust Him for the first time in his life. He asked him to lead the Israelites out of Egypt, away from the harsh oppression of King Ramses.

How many of you know that if a King is in power, he will not just let his slaves leave? I mean, who would be left to do the tasks that the Israelites were doing? Moses asked the King of Egypt multiple times to leave- ten to be exact. God used him to perform signs and wonders, from plagues of locusts, frogs, blood to finally killing all the first-born Egyptian males in the land. Pharaoh finally lets them go. Moses successfully led his people out of Egypt. And as he led them, we saw one of the best miracles God ever performed- the parting of the Red Sea. God moved and fulfilled His promise to Moses that He would get them out of Egypt safely.

It's important to note that Moses has a few reasons not to trust people: his mother threw him away when he was born, an Egyptian princess raised him in the palace while outside the palace walls, they oppressed his people, and his own people rejected him. I don't know about you, but those seem like pretty good reasons not to trust. Maybe you're like Moses, and you have gone through some not-so-nice things in your life. Many people in your life broke the trust between you, and now you find it easier to not trust at all than to try.

If Moses did not trust God, he would not have been successful. To step out in faith like that requires intimacy with the one asking you to go. It requires you to know who is sending you. When Moses chose to trust God, he saw some pretty remarkable miracles.

God is calling us to trust in Him. I believe we don't trust because we don't know the other person. If you are anything like me, you have a tendency to keep a wall up with people in your life. It's scary to be vulnerable with another human being. Even Jesus didn't trust certain people because He knew their nature; in fact, the Bible says that "He knew their hearts" (John 2:24-25). He knew who was for Him and who was against Him. Remember the Bible also says that, "God is not a man, so he does not lie. He is not human, so he does not change his mind" (Numbers 23:19). God is trustworthy, and He is asking us to trust Him. Will you take the step of faith to grow in intimacy with God so that you can learn to trust Him? Join me as we explore what it means to truly trust God, the one who deserves all our trust.

CHAPTER 1

Don't Doubt in the Light

13
THE DOUBT/FEAR CYCLE

To understand the relationship between doubt, fear and trust, we need to look at what I call the Doubt/Fear Cycle. It goes like this: when you are waiting on something, you step out in faith, trusting God will come through. As you wait, you begin to doubt that it will happen. In response, you silence that doubt by speaking God's promises over your situation. Then you wait some more. Perhaps you start to fear that it will never happen. In response, you pray and declare more of God's promises until you're back into trusting God again. This cycle can keep you from experiencing the peace that Jesus came to give us here on earth. The peace that surpasses all understanding; a peace that guards the promise from God in your heart (Philippians 4:7).

We need to be careful with doubt. As we saw in the Garden, doubt quickly turned into fear and/or disobedience (Genesis 3). All it takes is someone coming along and questioning what we knew to be true as not being true. It's important to note here that God is not a God of confusion; He will always bring clarity and order to anything He is involved in (1 Corinthians 14:33).

When I was five years old, I dreamed what my wedding would look like and who I would marry as every little girl did. I knew every detail, even what my dress looked like. For those who were curious, it was white. Yep, that's all the details I cared about. Give me a break; I was only five! As I got older, that dream wedding turned into a dream marriage.

When I was a teenager, my plan was to get married and have four children by the time I was 25. When I turned 23 and didn't even know who I was, I quickly realized that that dream wasn't happening any time soon. Fast-forward to when I gave my heart to Jesus at 28.

I put marriage on the shelf again because I wanted to focus on my relationship with God. Four years later, after I said yes to Jesus, I thought I was finally in a good place and ready to get married. Little did I know that God had different plans. By the time you read this book, I would have just turned 40, and I still dream of getting married.

I struggled with doubt for years when waiting on my spouse. As time went on, I began to doubt (before I experienced fear) that I would never get married. I had a specific promise from God about my marriage and the man I would marry. Although I had a promise from God, doubt filled my mind. Unrequited love interests, failed attempts at online dating, and liking men that never really liked me back had me reeling into a place of discouragement and self-pity.

I was in my late 30's (when I first started writing this book) and had not dated someone in over ten years. As I got older and looked around, I didn't see many men my age. Slim pickings, as they say, lead to a downcast heart. Where was my husband? When would God send him? These thoughts filled my mind and took me to a dark place.

In my case, fear caused me to give up on my promise from God for marriage and place it on the shelf. This fear came from getting my hopes up about this area of my life and seeing nothing come from it. After not meeting anyone year in and year out, fear crept in. Yes, I know God has His perfect timing, but sometimes that fact can be hard to grasp in the wait. So yes, fear crept in, and I decided rather than hold on to a promise I was afraid would never come to pass, I would let it go, so I didn't have to feel the sting of an unfulfilled promise in my life. It's self-preservation 101. It's not how God wants us to live. He has more for us on the other side of our trust in Him. More on that later on.

I used to think that if I doubted God and His promises, I was sinning. I now see that doubt in my circumstances strengthened my faith in

I now see that

doubt

in my circumstances strengthened my faith in God's promises.

God's promises. It allowed me to press more deeply into God and choose to trust Him even more. Yes, I had to constantly remind myself of the promises God spoke over my life. I had to choose to focus my mind on God's truth (His Word) and not what my circumstances said (2 Corinthians 5:7).

You see, I was able to lay down before God all of my doubts, fears and discouragements over the years to take hold of His promises. Yes, it was a choice, and yes, I struggled from time to time. But the result was a peace that now guards my mind and heart as I continue to trust God in this season (Philippians 4:7).

GAINED IN DROPS, LOST IN BUCKETS

I am no stranger to experiencing cycles of fear and doubt when trusting God. I have learned to trust God in many seasons and situations in my life, whether I was displaced, moving into a new apartment, paying for a missions trip, or waiting for my future spouse. All these circumstances have taught me to trust God throughout it all.

At the end of 2019, God called me to go on a missions trip to Cambodia. The trip was going to cost almost $4000. When I prayed about it, I felt God say that I was going. I didn't have the funds to go on this trip, which was three months away. Typically, you would get 6-8 months to fundraise and plan your trip, so it didn't give me much time to fundraise when God told me I was going. But the short timeframe also meant there was no time to doubt that God was going to come through. The first payment was due two weeks from when I submitted my application of interest. I did what any good Christian woman would have done. I prayed and asked God how He wanted me to fundraise.

I felt God give me Psalm 46:10, which says, "Be still and know that I am God." You see, I am a doer. I like to take action when I know there is something to do. I don't always take my time to plan and strategize before I act. That hasn't always worked out in my favour. However, I knew I had to act fast in this scenario as I had two weeks to fundraise for the first payment of just under $1000.

When I finished praying, I looked at my phone, and there was an email from Facebook for a new feature they had just launched. It was called Facebook fundraising. I did as much research as I could about it and learned what I was able to, and two days later, I launched my first Facebook Fundraising page. Since it was a new platform on Facebook, I committed to sharing it every day on my wall. Now that took BIG trust in God on my part- trust that He would come through and provide. Until this point in my life, I trusted God with more minor things over time, and He showed up. So, I had to trust him with something more significant.

"The Lord is my strength and shield. I trust him with all my heart, He helps me, and my heart is filled with joy. I burst out in songs of thanksgiving" (Psalm 28:7, NLT). When I prayed about how I would fundraise, I asked God if I could have all the money come in before the first payment was due at the beginning of December. God provided; He made it possible. Not only did I fundraise the total amount, but it all came in before I had to submit my first payment. Even in my season of lack, I was able to go on a missions trip. I flourished in this season. I chose to trust God, and He came through.

Have you ever heard the quote by Michael Todd that says, "Trust is lost in buckets and earned back in drops?" It merely means it's easy to lose trust in something/someone and is more challenging to gain it back. When trust breaks, it takes time to get it back.

I found this quote inverted to say, "Trust is earned in drops, and lost in buckets." It takes time to trust anyone when you first meet them. Trust requires vulnerability and comfortability. I mean that we should take our time learning to trust others. We won't necessarily be comfortable with everyone we meet off the bat, so it's okay to feel them out and learn to trust them bit by bit.

This is what our faith journey with God is like. When you first accepted Jesus into your life, did you trust every word of the Bible and everything God told you? No, you questioned and doubted and waited for proof to see if He was who He said He was. It happens over time as God shows up again and again in our lives. This process can take more time for those of us who have had trust broken repeatedly. Despite learning to trust God, I still have issues trusting Him sometimes. And that's okay; the point is to learn to trust Him. That's all He wants from us.

QUESTIONING SELF

Doubt was a firm companion of mine and usually stopped me from doing many things in my life. I suffered from low self-esteem from as far back as I could remember. It made me doubt everything around me, including what I did and said. Because I didn't trust myself in a situation, I allowed doubt and fear to hold me back. Unfortunately, I trusted the low self-esteem over myself. It was my most intimate companion until I met Jesus.

Another word of self-esteem is "self-respect." [iv]. So, when you have low self-esteem, it means that you don't respect yourself very well.

Another definition of self-esteem says, "a favourable opinion of oneself"[v]. People who have low self-esteem don't look favourably upon themself. They usually self-reject before others can reject them, talk negatively to or about themselves and almost always judge themselves very harshly. Sad to say that up until very recently, I did all of that.

For me, low self-esteem came from past trauma I experienced as a child. As a result, I learned that I had no value or worth, so why should anyone respect me. Because of what happened, I learned to reject who God made me to be. It made me doubt His creation and doubt how He created me. I even rejected my own appearance. I went from a young girl who used to model to someone who couldn't stand the sight of herself in a mirror.

Over the last few years, God has taken me through a process where He has begun to show me who I am. He has spoken words over me about who I am and who I am created to be, like:

> **Psalm 139:14**
> I will praise You, for I am fearfully and wonderfully made;
> Marvelous are Your works,
> And that my soul knows very well (NKJV).

Psalm 139:16
You saw me before I was born. Every day of my life was recorded in your book. Every moment was laid out before a single day had passed (NLT).

Ephesians 2:10
We have become his poetry, a re-created people that will fulfill the destiny he has given each of us, for we are joined to Jesus, the Anointed One. Even before we were born, God planned in advance our destiny and the good works we would do to fulfill it (TPT).

These verses began to reshape the way I saw myself, the narrative I was telling myself. I began to see who God created ME to be and not compare that with anyone else. Doubt started to melt away in the presence of God's truth. I began to trust who God created me to be and not who I thought I was. As I began to lay down the wrong thinking I had about myself and trust that God doesn't create junk, decision-making became easier; there was less doubt in my life. For the first time I can remember, I was free to be unapologetically ME and walk in that confidence.

So how do we conquer doubt to walk into all that God has for us? How do we continue forward in the face of doubt? The answer is simple, truth. Knowing the truth and trusting in God's truth about who He says we are.

"Doubt isn't the opposite of faith; it is an

element of faith"[vi]. Doubt can be a great tool to test and strengthen our faith. Are you facing a lifeless situation? Like me, are you still waiting for your spouse, hoping that God will finally help them find your address? Well, will you take the journey with me to choose to trust God in your season of waiting? Choose to face the question of 'Why am I still here?' in the face, and choose to trust God anyway? Most of all, let's be obedient and do the things He is asking us to do. Because, after all, we live for Him, to glorify Him.

CHAPTER 2

Trust is a Choice

WHY IS TRUST SO HARD?

So why is it so hard to trust? The answer lies in the Old Testament meaning of the word. To be vulnerable and transparent enough to let your guard down 100% of the time with someone. That's some risky business.

To understand what genuine trust looks like, we should look at vulnerability – "the condition of being laid open to something undesirable or injurious."[vii]. Vulnerability is opening yourself up to the point where you risk getting hurt. Have you ever been hurt before? I definitely have. However, our pain can be an aspect of how we learn. Suppose we aren't vulnerable, then we will never get hurt. But if growth comes from pain, then shielding our lives from pain and the beauty of vulnerability is false protection. God is calling us to something higher. He's calling us to trust Him with our hearts, to risk it all, to be vulnerable with others. You see, when we walk in trusting the Lord, we begin to experience miracles in our lives as we saw with Moses.

Quite frankly, I was surprised when God asked me to write a book on trust. I would be the last person to write about this topic by proxy of my past. However, here I am, and I believe that I will grow in this area as I write.

When I first came to Jesus, I had trust issues. I didn't trust anyone, not even myself. I was bitter and hurt and wanted to stay there because it felt comfortable. Early on in my walk, God challenged me to trust him one day. I remember what he said to me, "It's time to start trusting me." I broke down immediately and began to sob. Not the pretty tears that stroll down your face type-of-cry, but an all-out Kleenex-hungry sob fest. I then began to list all the reasons I didn't trust anyone. I didn't know God that well, so why would I trust Him? I didn't have an extended track record with God coming through at that point of my life.

In Genesis 32, Jacob is making his way back to the land of Canaan after working for his Uncle Laban for 20 years. As Jacob knew his twin brother, Esau, lived in Canaan, he sent gifts ahead to soothe Esau's anger. You see, Esau was the brother from whom Jacob stole his birthright and their father's firstborn blessing. So, it was understandable that he thought that he would be mad. He sent three sets of groups ahead of him with gifts for Esau.

Jacob admits in verse 11 that he was afraid that Esau was coming to attack him along with his wives and children. All of this after God told him to return to the land of his father and that he will treat him kindly. Due to sibling rivalry, Jacob could have chosen not to trust God or return to the land promised to him. But he decided to trust the God of his ancestors and go forth. It ended up that Esau was not mad at him and was so happy to be reunited with his twin brother.

In the Old Testament, God rarely showed Himself to people. In the next chapter of Genesis, Jacob sees God face to face and lives to tell the tale. Talk about intimacy. Everything people did in the Old Testament was done by faith. Most people never saw God or encountered Him. They made ritual sacrifices to Him regularly and prayed and tried to follow the law. They trusted God based on prior knowledge and stories passed down from generations about who God was and how He came through. Jacob only knew what his father told him and how God chose to manifest Himself.

It is okay to struggle with trusting God, especially if you have been through a lot in your life. When God got a hold of me, He knew that I needed to learn to trust Him if I wanted to see His will carried out in my life. I wanted to experience miracles. The point to focus on here is not how hard it was, but that I took the step of getting to know God more intimately so I could learn to trust Him - to be vulnerable with Him.

DON'T LET FEAR GUIDE YOU

The Bible contains the words "fear not" 103 times. The actual word "fear" appears in the King James Version of the Bible over 500 times [viii]. Fear is a real thing, and we see many people in the Bible face, struggle with, overcome and push through it to achieve their mission. It's not easy, and that's why God needs to remind us over 100 times not to fear. He promises that He is with us (Isaiah 41:10).

Years after Jesus ascends to heaven, Peter and his apostles are arrested. When they are taken in front of "all the rulers and elders and teachers of religious law" (Acts 4:5), the council questions them by what power and whose name they have healed a man (Acts 4:7). They respond in verses 8-12, saying this,

> Rulers and elders of our people, are we being questioned today because we've done a good deed for a crippled man? Do you want to know how he was healed? Let me clearly state to you all the people of Israel that he was healed by the powerful name of Jesus Christ the Nazarene, the man you crucified by whom God raised from the dead. For Jesus is the one referred to in the Scriptures, where it says, 'The stone that you builders rejected has now become the cornerstone.' There is salvation in no one else! God has given no other name under heaven by which we must be saved (NLT).

The council let them go because they had no evidence to keep them. Peter was a man who stood up for his faith, not because he loved confrontation. If you remember, this was the same Peter who denied Jesus three times after telling Him he would never do that to his face (Luke 22: 54-62). He did it because he trusted God to protect him and be with him.

Peter was the rock upon which God would build his church (Matthew 16:18). Peter was an integral part of building the new church AD. Therefore, he couldn't allow fear for his life to stop him from his mission. He was placed in prison three times, flogged, and had angels supernaturally free him from prison twice. He faced the fear of being stoned to death because of merely talking about Jesus publicly. But none of that stopped him. His mission was clear; help people find and follow Jesus.

Even during persecution, people were added to the number of believers daily. His mission was successful, but what kept him going despite facing fear daily? Peter knew his why, helping many souls get saved. It would propel anyone. But where does his mission come from? God. To work for the mission and sacrifice everything for it, you need to trust that the one who gave you the mission will help you fulfill it. You would even be willing to face all your fears to see it be successful.

When we allow

trust

to truly guide our lives, we open ourselves up to see the miraculous.

"Faith is trusting in the good. Fear is putting your trust in the bad"[ix]. This quote shows us that when we choose fear over faith, it's choosing to trust in the bad. If Peter had done this, he would have never seen many people come to Jesus.

I used to be a person that found it hard to believe in the good in my life. I had seen so many bad things happen that I always had a foreboding feeling something lurked around the corner. It was easy to believe in bad things because I had a track record of them happening in my life. I realize now that I was living in fear, and it guided every part of my life.

But today, I write as a woman who has shed the spirit of fear in her life and am learning to embrace trust in God to fulfill the mission He has given me. Writing this book is one of those steps. Sharing my story is another. So, what is it that God is asking you to do? Could it be those dreams that you dreamed a long time ago, but fear held you back from pursuing? Whatever it is, can I encourage you not to let fear guide you? When we allow trust to truly guide our lives, we open ourselves up to see the miraculous.

WHEN TRUST AND FEAR COLLIDE

I was petrified of dogs when I was a little girl. I would run away and hide from them whenever I saw them. I would even hide behind my parents if one was around. I didn't like them. You see, the thing was that I was afraid of anything that moved. I was more scared of animals because I couldn't communicate with them, and their movements were random to me. I liked to control things, and I couldn't control how they would move or what they would do, nor could I predict it.

An incident happened that changed my mind about dogs. I was ten years old, and I remember it like it was yesterday. It was the first time I was forced to face my fear of dogs. I was in the park one day after school with our after-school teacher. She had just got a new puppy and convinced me to hold him, to help me overcome my fear. Not two seconds later does a black Labrador dog come barreling towards me. I was petrified, and I didn't know what to do. My instinct at that moment was to protect that little dog I was holding from the big mean dog that was coming my way. I lifted up the dog and closed my eyes with the hopes that the big dog would go away. But, no, he did not, and he started jumping all around me like I was playing a game with him. I remember my teacher telling me to stand still. I have never stood more still in my life. I was scared.

The owner finally came and got the black Lab, only to find out later that he too was a puppy and just wanted to play with the puppy I was holding. Apparently, Labrador dogs grow very fast from when they are born, so they can be large even as puppies. Hence all of his jumping and playfulness. I remember thinking to myself, that was the first time I stood my ground in the presence of a dog and survived. After that, I had a new confidence when it came to dogs. I realized that dogs aren't that bad after all.

This is a simple illustration of overcoming fear in my life and how vital trust is in overcoming our fears. At that moment, I chose to trust what my teacher said to me, that the dog could not hurt me. Plus, I needed to rise to the occasion to protect the little dog I was holding, as I thought he was in danger. I chose to trust that the bigger dog had no power over me. Amidst our fear, God calls us to do the same thing. It can be easy when we are afraid to give in to fear and believe that our fears will overtake us. Yes, it takes bravery to trust in something else when we are scared. It takes courage to stand up to what makes us afraid and trust God that we will be alright.

Joshua was a man that was well acquainted

with fear. Moses was on his death bed, and God commanded him to anoint Joshua as the next leader. It comes when the Israelites are about to acquire the Promised Land for the first time since they sent out spies into the land 40 years ago. Also, Moses was one of the last prophets for a while whom God spoke face to face (Deuteronomy 24:10). Joshua was left to make decisions by casting lots. (Casting lots was used in the Old Testament to render an impartial, unbiased decision. It could have been different types of sticks or stones cast down. Think of it like throwing dice today to make a decision) [x]. He couldn't just pray to God, and God would talk to Him, like Moses. Joshua is commanded to take the Promised Land but can only make critical decisions on which order to take the land and which land goes to which tribe by casting lots. Talk about pressure.

In Joshua 1, God sends this message to Joshua:

> Be strong and courageous, for you are the one who will lead these people to possess all the land I swore to their ancestors I would give them...Be strong and very courageous...This is my command- be strong and courageous! Do not be afraid or discouraged. For the Lord your God is with you where you go (Joshua 1: 6-7, 9, NLT).

In the face of those enemies, Joshua had a choice to make, give in to his fears or trust that God would see him through and allow that to be the loudest voice he hears in his head.

God repeats these words three times "be strong and courageous." Why did you think that is? It's because He knew that Joshua would face some pretty scary stuff. There would be moments where he would face fear. In the face of those enemies, Joshua had a choice to make, give in to his fears or trust that God would see him through and allow that to be the loudest voice he hears in his head.

It's in the presence of fear that we truly learn to press in and trust God.

I believe that the feeling of fear can strengthen our trust in God. A little fear can test our trust. It's in the presence of fear that we truly learn to press in and trust God. It forces us to learn to trust that God is working all things together for our good. We learn to trust that God has our best interest at heart whatever we are going through. We learn to trust that God wants to give us good things only (James 1:17). We also learn to trust that He has plans for our lives, to give us a future and a hope (Jeremiah 29:11).

So, do you ever face the fear that you won't

ever get married? Do you face the fear that you will never meet your future spouse? Do you face the fear that God may not want you to have a spouse? I have faced all these fears and more when it comes to my single life. However, I have learned that it takes courage to trust God for the impossible. Just like God called Joshua to be strong and courageous, He calls each of us in our season of waiting to have the courage that God will bring our spouses in His perfect timing, and it will not be delayed (Habakkuk 2:3).

A. B. Simpson said, "Every fear is distrust, and trust is the remedy for fear." I read this quote, and it got me thinking that if trust is the remedy of fear, why don't we learn to trust more? Well, that is easier said than done. However, imagine what your season of waiting could look like if you mustered all the courage within yourself to trust God for his best? I believe that's where we would see fear and trust collide. And at that moment, our trust would begin to grow as our fears diminish. We would be left with a tested trust in God that has learned to stand under pressure.

TRUST IN THE MIDST OF FEAR

I believe to step out and do anything in fear, it takes trust in God to see you through it.

Joyce Meyer coined the term, "Do it afraid." Have you ever heard of this phrase? The term refers to doing something that makes you afraid, whether or not you have overcome your fear. That is what God calls us to do: trust Him amidst our fear. When we are scared, we are making a conscious decision to trust God that we will be able to do what he has called us to do. I believe to step out and do anything in fear, it takes trust in God to see you through it.

Six years ago, I adopted the term "do it afraid" as a sort of motto for my life. One day the Holy Spirit told me to sign up for online dating. At first, I was a little leery because I had heard horror stories of friends who had done it, and I didn't want any of that. Then I took some time to pray and think through what being online would look like. The first thing that rose up inside me was fear. It wasn't just that I was scared; I recognized that it was a deep-rooted fear. A fear that had stopped me from living my life before. I was scared to put myself out there. What if I got rejected? What if I didn't meet anyone? What if I met someone and then he broke my heart? Every "what if" scenario went through my head. Also, at that moment, I knew that I didn't want fear to stop me from doing anything anymore. You see, fear was a stronghold in my life. I allowed fear to hold me back from stepping out from a young age. Not any longer. I was determined to look fear in the eye and do it anyway. I did it. I signed up for a reputable site for over a year. I had conversations with catfish, marriage proposals, foreigners who just wanted permanent residency, you name it. Suffice to say that I didn't meet my husband on that site.

Afterwards, I thought it was a big waste of time. But then I realized that I learned to trust God even deeper by choosing to do something that made me afraid. I trusted God to keep me from falling for liars, to protect me from those who wanted to harm me and to keep my heart safe from those men that just weren't for me. So, although it wasn't the best experience, I grew through that experience. (Side note: God may ask you to go online to develop a character trait in you that wouldn't otherwise develop in any other environment.) Although I thought I was ready to meet my future husband, I was more grateful for the growth.

The way we lessen fear in our lives is to embrace God's love for us. To embrace God's love in our lives, we need to trust the giver of that love.

I read this quote from Saloni Verma that says, "Trust and fear are often related. Where there is fear, there will be less trust. If you want to create trust, then reducing fear is an important activity."

The only way to truly reduce fear is through love. 1 John 4:18 states that "there is no fear in love; perfect love drives out all fear" (GNTD). Love and fear cannot co-exist. The way we lessen fear in our lives is to embrace God's love for us. To embrace God's love in our lives, we need to trust the giver of that love. As we learn to trust, we begin to understand that all things, the good and bad, work together for our good.

Was there a time God asked you to trust him? Journal your experience.

JOURNAL

DO
OD
LE
IT!

Is there a promise from God that you are holding onto? Draw it in God's hand above.

QUESTION

Is there a situation in your life that you have traded trusting in God for trusting in yourself?

CHAPTER 3

What It Means to Trust God

TRUST OVER YOUR CIRCUMSTANCES

It's easy when waiting on God to do something in our strength or provide something with our resources. Our trust may start to wane at that point. We all are waiting on God to do something in our lives. Whether that's a new job, a better job, a baby, a spouse, financial breakthrough, relational breakthrough, no matter what you're waiting for, it takes a great deal of trust to see it through to the end and get your blessing.

I remember when I was between homes. I was on move #4 in the last five years of my life. I moved from place to place through a series of events until I found one I liked—kind of like Goldilocks and the "many homes." The place I was moving from was not my "just right" home. I was faced with a bachelor apartment to pack up and nowhere to go.

Fortunately, a friend from high school had a basement apartment that they were not currently using, so she allowed me to stay there. To say I was appreciative is an understatement. In my mind, I was as good as homeless. The Holy Spirit reminded me of a Scripture that said:

> And this same God who takes care of me will supply all your needs from his glorious riches, which have been given to us in Christ Jesus (Philippians 4:19, NLT).

God provided for me in this situation; however, my friend's basement apartment was not my "just right" home either. It's important to note that I'm not a fan of bugs.

Imagine this. You wake up to this eery feeling in the middle of the night to shine your iPhone 6s flashlight on the wall behind your bed to see multiple centipedes crawling above your head. Your first reaction is maybe this is all a dream. You pinch yourself and realize it's your reality. You finally fall back to sleep. The following day, you silently tiptoe into the bathroom to get ready in the hopes that you will not catch a glimpse of one of your little friends. Phew, you made it through brushing your teeth. You sneak into the living room to do your devotionals, and from the corner of your eye, you see a massive bug crawling up the wall. You throw something at it in the hopes it will disappear. It scurries across the wall. Then you notice something scurry along the floor across the room, so you fold your legs on the couch and pray you don't see anymore.

I wouldn't say it's the first time I have dealt with creatures and critters, but I don't do well with them. Add to that, I didn't want to overstay my welcome with my friend, because after all, she was giving me her basement apartment rent-free while I lived there! Blessed!

So here I was again, searching for a new apartment. Now I don't know about anyone else, but apartment hunting is one of the most stressful things that one can do. You see the perfect place online, whichever website you choose to use. Then you get excited, call them and either it's a scam, or you end up seeing the place, and the photos posted are from a year ago when it was just renovated—such a letdown. I didn't know how many apartments I saw like that until I found the perfect "just right" apartment. It was a one-bedroom, newly renovated in the colour scheme I wanted in a three-storey walk-up. Yes, that's how detailed I got when asking God for a place. (Side note: When I say I asked God, He challenged me to dream big when it came to an apartment and make my requests known to Him. Boy, did He ever come through!)

This apartment was the perfect place for me; however, there was a caveat. It wasn't out of my budget, but it was definitely on the high end of my budget. I knew that I would give up some of my financial freedom if I lived there. I wouldn't be able to save as much, but I would have my peace of mind. I had been in some unfortunate living situations in the past and was ready to live independently. This place would allow it. I had a choice, to trust that God would provide or wait it out in the centipede-infested basement apartment until something better came along.

I decided to get the apartment, and the way that happened, read God all over it. I forgot to mention that this place was in the downtown centre, with access to buses, parks and restaurants. It was in a great walkable and safe-to-walk-at-night neighbourhood. Of course, many people came to see the apartment and applied. I remember hesitating on applying because I was scared. I didn't want to be in a difficult financial situation. I decided to put in an application, and on the last date, applications were being accepted. I received a call. I think it was the Monday after I put in my application. She asked me about my place of work. I work for my church, and she talked about how she used to go there. And then she told me the apartment was mine!

I lived in that "dream" apartment for three and a half years. The peace I felt being on my own and doing what I wanted to do for the first time in my life was so precious. There is no price tag for that. God knew that I needed that peace in my home life. Yes, there were times when money was a little tighter, and I had to stay in

We have the choice to either *trust* God and receive the peace that comes along with that or to not trust Him and suffer our way through walking out His will for our lives.

when I maybe wanted to go out, but God always provided. I never lacked what I needed. He taught me how to budget, save my money and be responsible for a place of my own. He taught me to trust Him in a more significant measure than if I was in a home within my comfortable budget. I learned to trust God in my finances, which I had struggled to do up to that point.

When God pushes us out of our comfort zone, it takes trust to go willingly. We have the choice to either trust God and receive the peace that comes along with that or to not trust Him and suffer our way through walking out His will for our lives. I don't know about you, but I will always choose to trust God. He never fails or leaves us (Hebrews 13:5). Amidst my waiting and the uncertainty, I had to choose to trust God in the unknown. To trust God with things I had never trusted Him with before.

There are many examples in the Bible of people who trusted God. Shadrach, Meshach and Abednego were great examples of trusting God. Daniel 3 starts with King Nebuchadnezzar erecting a golden statue. He commanded the whole country of Babylon - including the exiled Israelites, to worship his statue whenever they heard "the sound of the horn, flute, zither, lyre, harp, pipes and other musical instruments" (v. 5). They had to stop what they were doing immediately and worship the king's statue.

Shadrach, Meshach and Abednego served only one God and worshiped one God. They refused to worship an idol here on earth. The king's astrologers found out, telling the king about them. They reminded them that Nebuchadnezzar would throw them into a fiery furnace if they didn't worship the statue. King Nebuchadnezzar brought them in and gave them one more chance to bow down to the statue. They refused, of course, and they were thrown into the fiery furnace.

At this point, if I were Shadrach, Meshach or Abednego, I would be panicking. Doubt would have settled in as to whether I did the right thing by standing up to the king. Their response here is crucial. They said in verse 16: "O Nebuchadnezzar, we do not need to defend ourselves before you. If we are thrown into the blazing furnace, the God we serve can save us. He will rescue us from your power, Your Majesty."

We must remember that our circumstances are only as big as we make them and that God is always bigger.

They trusted in their God, the all-powerful God. The God who is our Promise Keeper, our great Defender. Sure, they could have looked at their situation as a dead end. They disobeyed the king, and now they were being punished. They knew God, the great King of kings whom they served. In view of God, their circumstances shrunk. It was no longer as bad as they thought. God saved them from the fiery furnace. The flames did not singe them, and their clothes didn't even smell like smoke! That's the God we serve. That's the God we need to learn to trust in more. We also need to remember that our circumstances are only as big as we make them and that God is always bigger. We serve an awesome God.

TRUST IN GOD'S CHARACTER

At the age of 86, God spoke to Abraham that he would have a son and that his descendants would be as numerous as the stars in the sky (Genesis 15:5). After God tells him that, in Sarah's impatience, she tells Abraham to sleep with her servant, Hagar, who bears an illegitimate child from him. She did this right after she heard the promise from Abraham about his descendants being numerous. It was clear through her actions that she didn't trust God.

Later on, in Genesis, we see God tell Abraham that Sarah will bear a son for him in her old age. Sarah was 90 years old when God said this. At this point, she was under the impression that she was barren and could not give birth to children. In Genesis 18, three men of God tell Abraham that Sarah would give birth to a child. She overhears their conversation and laughs to herself, questioning how an older woman who has never had children before could have a baby. And from a man who was past his child-bearing days as well.

The difference between Abraham and Sarah was that he knew God. He saw God face to face and had conversations with Him. He walked with Him and grew in intimacy with Him. So, when the men of God told Abraham that he would have a natural heir through Sarah, he may have wondered how it would happen, but he trusted the God of Heaven's Armies to come through. He knew God could do anything. Abraham knew God's character.

Abraham trusted a God who was a provider, a protector, a multiplier, and a blesser. God often called Abraham to go, and He provided for him. He protected him from the Egyptians and gave him favour with King Abimelech (Genesis 20:14-15). He ensured that he and his household were always cared for and had enough land to grow crops to feed everyone.

Do you know the character of God? What would you say if someone asked you to describe who God was? One of His character traits is that He is trustworthy. The definition of trustworthy is someone who is "worthy of being trusted; dependable"[xi].

"The works of his hands are faithful and just; all his precepts are trustworthy" (Psalm 111:7, NKJV). Trusting that God is someone we can depend on is our responsibility as His children. When He says something will happen, we can trust Him because He is worthy of our trust. That trust comes from a place of God having a track record of always coming through and knowing God's character.

According to physicians, I am past my child-bearing years and considered high risk. I received a word from God eight years ago that I would get married and bear children. I have had a vision for my life - for my own family for quite some time. I write this book today, still single. Before you start feeling sorry for me, please don't. These have been some of the best years of my life. I got to grow with God exponentially. I had the chance to travel on missions trips worldwide and give everything I could to further the Kingdom. I wouldn't change a thing.

However, every year I'm reminded about that dream I have. As this dream was too hard to hold onto, I laid it down over the years. I am ashamed to say that I have even let it go and stopped feeding that dream. Recently, I had a revelation from God about who He is. He is a promise keeper. God doesn't live on earth; His mind works differently from ours. When He says He will do something, or it will happen in our lives, He says this with eternal and infinite knowledge. Therefore, we can be sure that He cannot and will not change His mind. After all, God's thoughts are higher than our thoughts (Isaiah 55:8). He doesn't make a promise and then breaks that promise like people. We already know that promises take time to manifest. During the waiting, I have a choice to make; let go of that dream and let it die, or refuse to let it go and hold on to it until I receive it in my life. You have that same choice, to hold or not to hold.

Let me warn you, holding onto a promise from God is not easy. It requires a strength of mind and spirit and a solid sense of who you are in Christ. All these things help you weather the storm while you wait on your promise. But, you know what? God provides grace for you during your season of wait, so it's not always hard.

Sure, there will be people who receive the same blessing you have been waiting for before you. Our job at those moments is to celebrate with those who celebrate (Romans 12:15). You have to remember that there will be a day when people celebrate with you.

You see, I know God as a promise keeper, but I also know him as an author (of my love story), a miracle worker, an all-powerful way maker who is faithful. I recognize the character of God because of my relationship with Him. So, when my natural eyes see a lack of potential suitors around me, I can choose to put my trust in a God who has a track record of keeping his promises. I can choose to trust in God entirely and rely on Him with all my heart. He provides for me, works out miracles in my life, makes a way where there doesn't seem to be a way, and remains faithful to me through everything.

> *My job is to trust my heavenly Father with the problems and situations I don't understand, and focus on stewarding my will to what I know to be true.* - Bill Johnson

Our job is to trust God even when we don't understand what is going on and steward what we know to be true. I know that I am single. I know that I have more time to go all-in for the kingdom of heaven. I know that I can be growing in the gifts and talents that God has given me. I know that I can spend more time becoming the right person before meeting the right person. If you're single, too, check out the resource page at the back of my book for some great resources to help you steward this season well.

TRUST IN GOD, NOT MAN

Earlier, we looked at what the word trust in Hebrew meant, but now let's look at the meaning of trust in the New Testament Greek. The Greek word for trust is *pepoithesis*. It means to have persuaded someone. It derives from the verb *peitho*, which means to trust and shows up 52 times in the New Testament [xii]. This type of trust requires prior knowledge of the person to accept what they say. This type of trust places the onus on the other person to persuade or convince us to put our confidence in him. This type of trust promotes a mindset of "prove to me that you are trustworthy before I trust in you." To trust someone this way, you need to have the whole picture of what is happening.

We see at the beginning of the book of Luke the story of Zechariah and Elizabeth. They were an older couple. Elizabeth could not conceive and therefore knew she wouldn't give Zechariah any children. But then God chose to bless her in her old age with a baby boy.

Here is a little background on where Zechariah and Elizabeth are at this time in their lives. Zechariah was a part of the priestly group of Abijah, who belonged to the tribe of Levi. In the book of Exodus, God appointed Levi's tribe to serve as priests in His temple and take care of it. Zechariah is deemed special as he was part of the original Levite priestly line. And Elizabeth is from the family of Aaron, also a Levite. So, this is a special couple who were going through pain. The culture at this time was that when couples couldn't have children, the blame was often placed on the wife's shoulders as she was the one who conceived. Furthermore, Jewish culture believed Zechariah and Elizabeth could not conceive because God was not pleased with them [xiii].

Our story begins with Zechariah in the synagogue doing his priestly duties. Suddenly, an angel of the Lord (Gabriel) appears to him and tells him that Elizabeth is pregnant with a son and that he is to name him John (v. 13). When this happened, Zechariah questioned how this would happen as he looked at his situation's reality (v.18). Both he and his wife were old, and Elizabeth could not conceive. The story continues with the angel trying to persuade Zechariah on behalf of God to believe the validity of what he said (v.19). Since Zechariah questioned Gabriel, he silences him, and he cannot speak until the baby is born.

Zecharaiah and Elizabeth were righteous people who were careful to obey all of God's laws. They did what was right in the eyes of God. God wanted to bless and use them within the narrative he wrote for his people. So, they both knew God very well. Zechariah spent most of his latter days in the temple of God, praying and worshipping. However, God needed to persuade him. That's why God sent the angel Gabriel. Gabriel says in verse 19, "I stand in the very presence of God." God didn't send any old angel; He sent one of the "three" angels.

The Bible talks about how the angel Gabriel stood in the very presence of God (Luke 1:19). So, God brought out the big guns to go down to earth and tell Zechariah that Elizabeth was about to conceive a child. Even with all of that, Zechariah needed persuading. After living a long life and giving up on that dream, he most likely put it to rest. When Zechariah met Gabriel, a being Zechariah had never seen or heard about, he doubted. He trusted in himself and his wife and the fact that they were old.

God calls us to trust in Him, Almighty God, King of Kings, Lord of Heaven's Armies, The Great I AM! No matter what is happening in our lives, no matter what we see in ourselves or others around us. God is bigger than all of that. God created each of us. Therefore, he can supernaturally move in ways that will blow us away. Of course, God could have Elizabeth conceive in her old age when she couldn't do so her entire life. That's who He is, and as the great Father He is, He will continue to persuade those who fear Him and are committed to His ways.

Is there a situation in your life where you have traded trusting in God for trusting in yourself and others around you? Oh, I can do this, I got this, all I need to do is! - Do those phrases sound familiar? As a single woman living in the 21st century, trusting in my talents, gifts, and abilities has become way too easy. The term "girl boss" is thrown around all over social media to symbolize having arrived, and you are working hard on your own to create a successful endeavour. Now, I'm not saying anything is wrong with that if that's your goal. You do you, Boo, and go get yours. However, there is a problem when the motive is that I trust in myself rather than God. When we do this, we take away the Father's right to try and persuade us to put our confidence in Him. We take away His joy of working things out for us miraculously. We steal His pleasure of blessing us unexpectedly. God wants us to trust Him because He knows that's where our blessing lies.

Psalm 20:7 says, "Some trust in chariots and some in horses, But we will remember and trust in the name of the Lord our God." David wrote this Psalm before he went into one of his many battles. It was more of a battle cry against his enemies. David was a man who trusted the Lord. He trusted Him in the Old Testament way because he pursued intimacy with Him. David also trusted God in the New Testament way. God convinced him that He would do what He said He would do. God persuaded him that He would come through all the time.

> *Trusting God is not a matter of my feelings, but my will.* - Jerry Bridges

Jerry Bridges says it ideally in his quote. Trusting God is a choice; it's a matter of my will. It's saying yes to God and no to my flesh. It's saying to God, I will trust You first every time I have to make a decision. No matter what is happening, no matter my circumstances, no matter how difficult or if it doesn't come naturally to me. I will choose to trust in You because there is no other choice as far as I'm concerned.

NO SIGN OF LIFE

Have you ever been in those situations where it looks like there is no life, no way out or no way through? Situations like those are breeding grounds for doubt. It's easy to doubt in the dark what God has spoken to us in the light [xiv]. Remember that the enemy uses doubt as a tactic to keep us from fulfilling our purpose here on earth. If the enemy can keep us doubting everything God says to us, he keeps us in a place of stagnancy, leading to frustration.

One of God's names is the Way Maker. That means when it looks like there is no sign of life in your situation, God comes through; He makes a way for you. That is God's character; it is who He is. God cannot help Himself but make a way. He parted the Red Sea so that His people could walk safely on dry land, He threw down the walls of Jericho so His people could overtake their Promised Land, and He even used a talking donkey to confuse the Israelites' enemies. The most important of them is that He made a way through His Son to bring us back into a relationship with Him. Part of trusting God is remembering who He is. Like we learned before, it's choosing to trust in His character over our situations.

There was a man in the Bible who doubted God. Gideon was one of the judges of Israel. At that time, Joshua, their leader, had just died, and they were still in the middle of acquiring the rest of the Promised Land. God implemented judges among his people to keep them in obedience. Unfortunately, they didn't listen to them and kept on sinning. So, God sent the Midianites to attack them.

In walks Gideon. He is going about his own business when an angel of the Lord appears and calls him "Mighty hero" (Judges 6:12).

Gideon questions the angel about where God is in all the Midianites are doing to his people. So, the angel replies to him and says this, "Go with the strength you have, and rescue Israel from the Midianites. I am sending you!" (Judges 6:14). Gideon doubts the angel of the Lord again, claiming that his clan is the weakest and questioning how God can even use them or him for that matter (Judges 6:15).

God ends up using Gideon, but not before He performs a couple of miracles for him and then strips his army of 20,000 down to just 300 men. They end up winning the battle against the Midianites with 300 men! That was a great miracle! We can learn a few things from Gideon when faced with a whole heap of doubt in what seems like a lifeless situation:

1. **God is still moving in your situation.** God promises us that he never leaves us or forsakes us (Hebrews 13:5). God is continually moving on our behalf, even if we can't see it. It is a choice to trust that in the face of what seems lifeless, nonetheless, it is truth. Hold on to it, and embrace it.

2. **God is in the business of miracles.** He can make a miracle in your situation. There is a song my church wrote called You are Here. A line of it says, "God you move in miracles" [xv]. The Holy Spirit revealed to me one day about

God as a miracle worker. He revealed that God is supernatural, and when he moves in a natural world, it manifests as a miracle. If God is always with us, that means miracles are happening all around us all the time. Let's trust God to see a miracle in our lifeless situation.

3. **God is a restorer!** That's who He is and what He does. God is in the business of restoring what was stolen or lost to us. God restored Job's fortunes and family to him after he suffered a significant loss (Job 42). God can restore your familial relationships; He can restore your self-confidence. And He can definitely restore your trust in Him. God wants to restore all the things you lost or were taken from you. He wants your latter days to be greater than your former (Job 8:7).

4. **Just because it looks lifeless on the surface doesn't mean that God isn't working.** A plant seems lifeless on the surface for the first week until the shoot begins to penetrate the soil, and you begin to see growth. Remember, your life can look like that from time to time, but something is always happening beneath the surface. Your life is not stagnant.

5. **Choose to move forward even in the face of death.** Gideon chose to move forward, although it seemed like an impossible task.

God wanted him and his army of 300 men to take on sophisticated armies of the powerful Midianites. But He swore to him that He would be with them and that He would give them victory. At that moment, Gideon chose to trust God over what he saw. He decided to step out boldly in that trust, and he got to see God move in his situation in a powerful way.

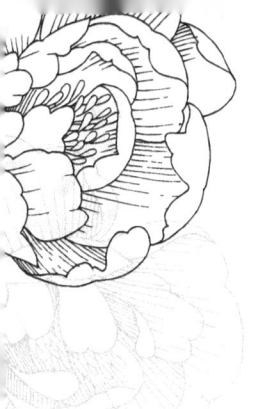

JOURNAL

Is there a situation in your life where you have traded trusting in God for trusting in yourself and others around you?

_____
_____
_____
_____
_____
_____
_____
_____
_____
_____
_____
_____
_____
_____
_____

QUES
TION

What did you learn from Gideon in his story in the Bible?

DOODLE IT!

Draw the different character traits of God that you can think of.

CHAPTER 4

Trust Is A Heart Issue

THE LOVE/TRUST CONNECTION

There is a special relationship between love and trust. To understand what it means to truly trust God, we need to look at love. In this chapter, we will take a closer look at love and its relation to trust.

C.S. Lewis came up with a way to classify the types of love experienced in life. In all, there are four types. The first is *storge* (or affection); the kind of love you feel about people you are familiar with, like your family. "Affection almost slinks or seeps through our lives," he says. "It lives with humble, un-dress, private things; soft slippers, old clothes, old jokes, the thump of a sleepy dog's tail on the kitchen floor, the sound of a sewing-machine"[xvi].

The second is *philia* (friendship), which refers to the love you have for your friends who are as close as siblings. We see this love in the Bible, in the bond between David and Jonathan. Although they weren't blood relatives, they were still extremely close and treated each other like brothers (2 Samuel 1:26). "We develop a kinship over something in common, and that longing for camaraderie makes friendship all the more wanted"[xvii]. It's a love that benefits from a bond over something you share with each other. "Lewis thinks friendship likely has the closest resemblance to Heaven where we will be intertwined in our relationships"[xviii].

The third is *eros* (romantic), the love we often see between lovers or husband and wife. Lewis explains this love as "in one high bound it has overleaped the massive wall of our selfhood; it has made appetite itself altruistic, tossed personal happiness aside as a triviality and planted the interests of another in the centre of our being. Spontaneously and without effort, we have fulfilled the law (towards one person) by loving our neighbour as ourselves. It is an image, a foretaste, of what we must become to all if Love Himself rules in us without a rival" [xix]. This love finds oneself wrapped up entirely in another being.

The last one is *agape* (charity). This love "exists regardless of changing circumstances;" it's a sacrificial love. This love is the unconditional love that God gives us" [xx]. (Check out my resource page for information on C.S. Lewis' book)

For the most part, most of us will experience all four types. Let's look at the story of Jonathan and David and the love they had for each other. When Jonathan met David, he had an instant bond with him. 1 Samuel 18:1 states, "There was an immediate bond between them, for Jonathan loved David."

In 1 Samuel 19, we see King Saul plotting to kill David. He was angry with David because he knew that David would succeed him as King. He urged his servants and his son, Jonathan, to kill David. Of course, Jonathan didn't want to do that at all because of his allegiance to David. That is the *philia* love on display right there. Verse 1 says, "But Jonathan, because of his strong affection for David, told him what his father was planning." So Jonathan betrayed his own father for David. That's huge.

That kind of intimacy comes from vulnerability with another person, which generally leads to love, whether that's *storge*, *philia*, *eros* or *agape*. I can picture Jonathan and David having late-night conversations about their hopes and dreams and worries about what will happen in the future. Maybe it wasn't only jealousy of David becoming King; perhaps it was jealousy that Saul didn't have that *storge* love he yearned for with his son? Maybe he was jealous of their *philia* love?

Have you ever met someone in your life, other than your spouse, and you just clicked with them? It seemed like you had so much in common the first time you met, and you could just talk for hours with them. You couldn't wait to spend time with them because they just got you. Trust was built quickly because of the intimacy between you early on in your friendship.

I have been blessed to have two people in my life like this. When we met, it was like we had known each other for years. After a couple of months of friendship, people would ask how long we had known each other because the bond we shared was apparent to others. We could talk for hours and about nothing and everything when we spoke. I don't have any sisters, so these friendships are special to me. They give me a place of shelter to be raw, honest and ultimately myself. There is no judgment from either side, and we love each other. If you are fortunate enough to have a friend or two like that, consider yourself blessed. This is *philia* love at its finest.

"There is no greater love than to lay down one's life for one's friends" (John 15:13). Remember the Old Testament definition of trust: to lay down on the ground before someone? This Scripture says that the greatest love - agape love takes the form of laying one's life down for someone else. So, in love and trust, it requires a laying down of self in some way, shape or form. Jesus was not expecting everyone to die for another when he said this. No, he was saying that there is no greater love than the love of Jesus, to die for the world - to lay down, the ultimate act of humility, his life for us. When we trust others, we need to lay parts of ourselves down. We must lay down pride, self-sufficiency and independence. We must risk being vulnerable enough to allow people to see us as we are and know they will be there for us. That's what trust is.

Agape love is the highest form of love that can only come from God. As mentioned above, this love is sacrificial; it's unchangeable, it's immovable. It can be easy to trust this type of love. When you know that someone has already sacrificed their life for you, how could you not be confident in laying your life down for them?

Unfortunately for me, it wasn't a comfortable journey to trust God. I knew God loved me, and He was for me, but experience showed me something altogether different. As I shared previously, trust was broken in my life many times before. I trusted some of these people to protect me, and they broke that trust. As a result, this experience taught me not to trust people. And rightly so, because I was hurt. That was added to by a tumultuous relationship with my mother. As a young girl who didn't get along with the only other female in her household, that was hard. I had to learn to trust God despite what my past was.

Jesus calls us to lay down our lives and take up his cross (Luke 9:23). That takes trust. To leave the life you have always known and follow

Jesus, a man you just met. This was not an easy feat for me. Earlier on in my walk with Christ, I would always be looking for moments in my life when things didn't go my way, to blame God. All I had known was let down and heartache, so why would this be any different? I was so wounded from my past experiences, and that was okay for God. I never understood why He loved me so much despite my flaws. But I know now, and it's incredible! He loves us just the way we are because that's how He created us to be. God has a plan for our lives despite our flaws, mistakes, and quirks, and He wants to use us in that plan. That is worth trusting in.

God has a plan for our lives despite our flaws, mistakes, and quirks, and he wants to use us in that plan.

MISTRUST STARTS IN THE HEART

> *Unlike people, God will never turn his back on you. Trust in him with all your heart, and you will never have to worry about being betrayed.-* Anonymous

Now that we see the connection between trust and love, we can understand how the heart plays into it all. What does it mean to trust in God with all your heart? What does that look like? I believe trusting God with all your heart is laying down your fear, insecurities, doubts, victories, hopes, dreams, wants, desires, future, your whole life, at His feet. Being able to say to

God, *Although I'm confused, I trust that you have my best interest at heart.*

You see, I was one of those people who would hide my feelings, my true feelings. When I came to Christ, I didn't like that He could see all of me. There were parts of me I wanted to hide from the whole world and never show anyone. I was anti-vulnerability. The least I had to show the world about the real me, the better it was for all involved. Mistrust came quickly to me because of what I went through as a child.

Mistrust means to lack trust in something [xxi]. To lack trust, there needs to be a root for why we don't or cannot trust. Usually, that root can lead us straight to a hurt we experienced in the past. Hurt happens in the heart - the seat of our will and emotions. Mistrust is us choosing to not put our heart into something. It can become like second nature for some of us to not let people or things into our hearts. However, God calls us not to allow our past to dictate our future. This is where healing needs to take place. Forgiving those who have wronged us is a big step in the right direction. Check out my resources page at the back of this book for some great resources about forgiveness.

I have learned that I get to control how much I allow someone into my heart.

> *Broken trust is a real and tragic relational consequence of someone's poor behaviour, especially when that same behaviour is repeated over and over again.* - Leslie Vernick

Have you been hurt over and over by the same person? I have. Like the good Christian woman I was, I forgave that person repeatedly because that's what the Bible says to do. There was a point in my life when I had to draw the line and not allow this person's reckless behaviour into my life anymore. I had to draw a boundary between that person and me. It wasn't easy. It was actually one of the most complex decisions I have ever made, but it was essential to my overall emotional health and well-being.

There is another way of living that allows us to step out of the mistrust cycle and truly start trusting God. Proverbs 4:23 says: "Guard your heart with all diligence because out of it flows the issues of life." Our real life, the life that God has called us to, lives in our hearts. This is where we feel pain, hurt, love, joy, desire, all feelings within our hearts. As I mentioned earlier, I find it hard to trust people. However, I have learned how to trust God over the years.

It's easier to

trust

someone when you know your
heart is protected.

I have learned that I get to control how much I allow someone into my heart. I practice guarding my heart every time I meet someone new. As they show me that they can be trusted, I can give them a bit more of my heart. Let me be clear that guarding your heart does not mean keeping everyone at arm's length and away from you. It doesn't mean to build up a wall around your heart so that no one can get in. No, guarding your heart is not letting every person you meet all the way in. It allows you to trust people by allowing them in your heart a little at a time until you feel safe enough to be completely vulnerable with them- lay yourself down in front of them. It's easier to trust someone when you know your heart is protected.

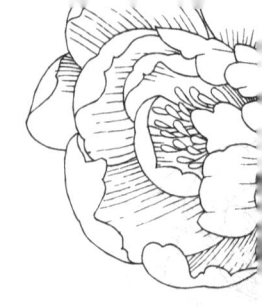

JOURNAL

Journal about the types of love that are present in your life. How do you relate to the agape love that God pours out on us?

QUESTION

Is there an area or multiple areas in your life where you mistrust God or people?

DO
OD
LE
IT!

Draw a graph of how much you experienced each type of love in your life.

CHAPTER 5

Trust Is Active

WHERE YOUR TREASURE IS...

"For your heart will always pursue what you value as your treasure" (Matthew 6:2, TPT). Understanding what this part of Scripture says is essential to understanding the heart/trust connection. If we know that our hearts are the seat of our mind, will and emotions, essentially, our whole life, we need to be cognizant that we are collecting the right kind of treasures. What are the correct types of treasures?

According to this translation of Matthew 6:21, a treasure is anything you place value in. Earlier in Matthew 6, it talks about two types of treasures; "Don't store up treasures here on earth, where moths eat them and rust destroys them, and where thieves break in and steal them. Store your treasures in heaven, where moths, rust cannot destroy, and thieves do not break in and steal" (NLT). Let's be clear that as Christians, Matthew is urging us to not focus on gathering earthly possessions or treasures; the biggest house, the nicest car, the most expensive boat, etc. Instead, he wants us to focus on collecting heavenly treasures. The treasure he refers to is good deeds, producing fruits of the Spirit in our lives, loving our neighbours, and trusting others. As I mentioned before, I want to learn to trust people, not for my own sake but to fulfill God's calling on my life.

What is your heart pursuing? I love how The Passion Translation states that your heart will pursue only those things you place value in. That's your treasure. The definition of pursue is: "to seek, or strive to attain." Another definition is "to follow persistently or seek to become acquainted with" [xxii]. Are you pursuing / striving/seeking/attaining/persistently following/ loving others over always being right? Are you striving for forgiveness over retaliation? Are you seeking to give rather than receive? Are you persistently following humility over pride? Are you striving to attain an attitude of gratitude rather than become rich? And are you seeking to trust others over choosing to distrust?

I ask you again, where is your treasure? Let's look at the Israelites and how they focused on the wrong thing in the wilderness. In Exodus 14, we read that God just delivered his people from the Egyptians. They walked on dry ground in the middle of the Red Sea with the waters parted like a wall on each side (v. 29). I don't know about you, but if God parted the seas for me, I would do my happy dance, post it on social media, scream it from the rooftops; everybody would know. I would worship God in such a grand way. Exactly how the Israelites worshipped Him.

How soon the Israelites forgot. Three days

after God saves them, they begin to complain to Moses. Three days! They couldn't even give it a week (Exodus 15:24). I mean, God just saved them and killed most of Pharaoh's army. They straight-up saw one of the biggest, most epic miracles in the history of God here on earth, but they decided to complain.

If we are honest with ourselves, there have been times where we have forgotten the blessing God just provided for us in the face of a new storm.

However, I can't judge them because I get it. If we are honest with ourselves, there have been times where we have forgotten the blessing God just provided for us in the face of a new storm. Sometimes it's easy to forget what God has done, the miracle that got you through when you're face to face with another giant. For the Israelites, that giant was hunger starvation. When faced with the potential to starve in the wilderness, they began to complain. They were focused on the wrong thing. Instead of focusing on how powerful God is and how He literally brought them through the Red Sea on dry ground, they were concentrated on their bellies.

Matthew 4:4 says that "man does not live by bread alone but by every word that comes from the mouth of God." It's so important to

When you learn to

trust

God, it's easy to believe the words
He is speaking to you.

focus on God at all times. Matthew is saying that yes, our bodies need food, but more importantly, we need intimacy with God. We need his life-giving Words. The Israelites needed to continue to focus on worshipping a God who was strong enough to deliver them from the hands of their enemy and less on the hunger they were feeling.

I know this is easier said than done. There is a way to get our hearts focused on the right thing, cultivating heavenly treasures as opposed to earthly treasures. Part of it is learning to trust God. When you learn to trust God, it's easy to believe the words He is speaking to you. It's easier to be vulnerable with Him, thus grow in intimacy with Him. When we go deeper in our relationship with God, we are bound to store up treasures in heaven. We begin to see the fruits of the Spirit manifest in our lives.

Remember, wherever our treasure is, there our hearts will be. So, where is your focus, on your circumstances or on God? Are you more concerned about growing a life filled with the fruits of the Holy Spirit or focused on your circumstances and feelings? Joel Osteen says it well in this quote: "When you're really believing, when you're in peace, you're showing God by your actions that you trust Him." Would you say that you are at peace in every area of your life? Do you trust God with your whole life, even the parts that may not be where you want them to be? Trust is being vulnerable and open with another person. Does God get your whole heart and life?

I know, this sounds scary. It is. However, it is worth it. I have learned to trust God over the years. It wasn't easy at first, but over time as He came through, I realized that that was the only way to live. God's promise for those who trust in Him is that He will keep them in perfect peace (Isaiah 26:3). Is there an area of your life where you lack peace? May I suggest that you aren't fully trusting God with that area of your life; you are not laying down in front of Him. My encouragement is to seek God in this area of your life. Allow the Holy Spirit to search your heart and point out to you those areas that are not surrendered to God. As you learn to trust with your whole life, I'm confident that you will begin to see the miracles that Moses and the Israelites experienced.

HIDE HIS WORD WITHIN YOUR HEART

When you go through a heart transformation, it's sometimes difficult to spot the change in someone's life right away. It takes time for what was done on the inside to manifest on the outside. Jesus put it plainly when he says, "A good tree produces good fruit" (Matthew

7:17, NLT). He was talking about how we must beware of false prophets. However, this can be extended to anyone who calls themselves a follower of Jesus. The fruit he is speaking about is the above-mentioned fruits of the Holy Spirit. We cultivate the fruits of the Spirit in our lives by getting the Word of God in us.

What does that look like? Reading your Bible every day, listening to the Bible or Bible-themed podcasts, watching or listening to sermons about the Word of God and memorizing Scripture. These are just some of the ways; there are many more I'm sure you can come up with. This is important because it fosters a relationship with God. How? God's Word is how we recognize His voice. I hear this saying all the time: 'Want to recognize the voice of God in your life? Then read His Word consistently.' The Bible is God's Word.

Once God changes our lives from the inside out, we need to ensure that change lasts as we learn to trust Him. One way we do that is by hiding His Word in our hearts. The Psalmist says in Psalm 119:11, "Your word I have treasured and stored in my heart, that I may not sin against you" (AMP). Again, God encourages the Israelites in Deuteronomy 6:6, "these words which I command you today shall be in your heart" (NKJV). Why would God ask His people to store His words in their hearts? Like we discovered earlier, it took God's chosen people three days to forget the miracles of being delivered from the hands of their enemies and seeing the Red Sea parted. When God gave His people the law, He wanted to ensure they never forgot it or stepped away from it. He knew that there were life and blessings in His laws. It wasn't for God's sake; it was for the sake of the Israelites. He knew life would be better for them if they continued to obey the law.

Then again, in Psalm 37: 31, David's words are paraphrased in The Message version; "His heart pumps God's Word like blood through his veins; his feet are as sure as a cat's." I believe what he is saying here is that knowing God's word so well with great intimacy will give you confidence in each step you take. Another version says that "their feet do not slip" (NIVUK). This is what trust in God looks like. Knowing God so intimately that you are confident in your life and in what God is doing in your life. Your feet are as sure as a cat's.

I'm not a big animal person; that's because I'm allergic to most things that have fur. This includes cats. However, I like to watch how cats move. They are curious animals that are so nimble on their paws. They say a cat has nine lives. I believe that's because cats aren't afraid to jump and leap onto and off things and surfaces. Cats are so sure of themselves, to the point where it seems they are willing to risk their lives. I'm not surprised that they have nine lives because they probably go through one of them every time they take a leap. Cats aren't afraid to take risks. David says that it makes our feet sure, secure, steady and strong like a cat's when we hide God's Word in our hearts. We aren't afraid to take risks knowing that God is for us. This is what trusting in God looks like.

Knowing the Word so well that it changes hearts in its presence when shared, sent or spoken.

When you are well acquainted with God's Word, that it's like blood pumping in your veins, you can't separate yourself from it. So, what does that actually look like in your life? Have you ever been in a challenging situation, and you find yourself remembering a Scripture that gives you a fresh perspective? Have you ever received a text from someone with a timely, encouraging word that brings you peace in your storm? Have you ever read your Bible and the words jump off the page and speak to your heart when you're going through a difficult situation? That is what knowing the Word of God personally looks like; knowing the Word so well that it changes hearts in its presence when shared, sent or spoken.

David was a man who knew the importance of hiding God's word in his heart. There is a popular Kids' ministry story in the Bible of David and Goliath. David, a 16-year-old teenager, takes on Goliath, a literal giant, and wins (1 Samuel 17). Our story starts with Jesse calling his teenage son, a shepherd, out of the fields to send him to deliver lunch to his brothers. They were on the frontlines in the war against the Philistines. We see Goliath taunting the Israelites and calling God names when he arrives. David is indignant by this, so he decides to confront the giant.

He is sent to the King and convinces King Saul to allow him to go and kill Goliath. David gears up to go into battle with him but is too small for the gear, so he arms himself with a slingshot and three smooth stones. As he goes to fight Goliath, David says this in 1 Samuel 17:45:

> You come to me with sword, spear, and javelin, but I come to you in the name of the Lord of Heaven's Armies- the God of the armies of Israel, whom you have defied. Today the Lord will conquer you, and I will kill you and cut off your head. And then I will give the dead bodies of your men to the birds and wild animals, and the whole world will know that there is a God in Israel! And everyone here will know that the Lord rescues his people, but not with sword and spear. This is the Lord's battle, and he will give you to us (NLT)!

Where did his confidence come from? Why was he so bold to speak out like that? David walked with God. David heard from God. His confidence came from knowing the King of Kings personally, the Lord of Heaven's Armies, who helped him defeat lions and bears. Back then, they didn't have a Bible to read. All they had to rely on was prayer - talking to God. As we see from the many Psalms David wrote throughout his life, God spoke to him. He learned to write down, memorize, and get the words God spoke to him in his heart. Sound familiar? Earlier, we talked about what hiding God's Word in your heart looks like? In the case of David, it looks like a victory in the face of the impossible.

Is there an area of your life where you need victory? Maybe you have been going around the same mountain over and over, and you just need a breakthrough? My next question to you is how well do you know God's Word? Is it like food to you that you feel the need to consume every day? Or is it more like I draw on it when I need it? One of my leaders always says that consistency is vital. One day when we are in a season of spiritual drought in our lives, we will need to draw on the well that we have created in our lives by consistently getting into the Word of God, praying and seeking His face. If you aren't at a place where this is you and you are either smack dab in the middle of your storm, or you're in a good place, start today. Start getting the Word of God into you. You won't regret it.

LET THE LIGHT SHINE THROUGH

> *Trusting God enough to guide us down the best pathway of our lives requires us to first surrender our life to Him.* -
> Heather Bixler

Now that we have examined why it can be challenging to trust and the different ways we can trust after heartbreak, let's look at how genuine trust is lived out. Like the quote above, this trust looks like surrender. This leads us back to the Old Testament definition of trust: to lay down on the ground in front of someone. Literally to lay down your life at that person's feet. Heather is asking us to humble ourselves enough that we lay all on the line for God. Are you willing to do that?

In the fourth chapter of the Book of Daniel, King Nebuchadnezzar has to learn to lay it all down at God's feet. He was the King of Babylon, the most powerful country in the world. He had just overtaken Israel and taken most of their people into captivity. However, pride got in the way, and he demanded everyone to bow down and worship a statue he erected whenever they heard specific instruments played (remember Chapter 3?).

Then King Nebuchadnezzar dreamed about a great tree that gets cut down to its stump. This is the beginning of the end for Nebuchadnezzar. After Daniel interpreted his dream, he warned the King to stop sinning and do what was right (v. 27). However, that doesn't stop the dream from being fulfilled. Nebuchadnezzar is driven from human society into the wilderness. After the prescribed time passes, Nebuchadnezzar looks up to heaven, praises and worships "the Most High and honored the one who lives forever" (v. 34). The chapter finishes with Nebuchadnezzar's Kingdom being restored.

I interpret that story in Scripture as God needing to take King Nebuchadnezzar on a journey of trusting Him. If he didn't have everything stripped from him, he would have never turned from his evil ways after being so powerful. He was literally put in a position where he had to choose whether or not he would surrender his life to God. He believed in God's Word as his dreams came true. So why did he decide to trust God after what he had been through? The answer is simple, he became acquainted with God. He grew in relationship with God. That's where his praise and worship came from.

Experience is the key that unlocks our hearts to trust in God.

This is important, you don't want to miss this. Experience is the key that unlocks our hearts to trust in God. Each time we experience God coming through on our behalf, He saves us from a more dire outcome and spares our life when we should have perished. It's those combined experiences, like with Nebuchadnezzar, that causes us to trust God more confidently. We slowly begin to learn to trust Him with each situation we face. As He comes through, steps in, protects and makes a way, we experience His true nature and realize that we can depend on Him.

What can we learn from Nebuchadnezzar on how to live a life of trust? Firstly, he humbled himself (Daniel 4:34). Nebuchadnezzar's first response when his sanity returned to him in the wilderness was to praise and worship God. He humbled himself by accepting God's will for his life. It was an act of surrender. He was showing God that he trusted his ways over his own.

Secondly, he honoured God (v. 34- 37). He honoured Him through song. Nebuchadnezzar's second response after his sanity returned was that he chose to give honour to God. His heart was now bent towards God, and his eyes were opened. He understood for the first time who God really was and the power that He possessed. He knew as a former king that you honour royalty, and that's what he was doing for God through his song.

Thirdly, he opened his heart to God. For him to be transformed, he had to be open to God. He no longer wanted to lift himself up, but immediately his heart wished to lift God up. He saw God's power at work in his own life, and he chose to open his heart up to Him. As a result, God restored him. I'm reminded of 1 Peter 5:10, which says, "And then, after your brief suffering, the God of all loving grace, who has called you to share in his eternal glory in Christ, will personally and powerfully restore you and make you stronger than ever. Yes, he will set you firmly in place and build you up." This is what happened to Nebuchadnezzar; he suffered for a brief time, and then he was restored. Is there an area of your life that needs restoration? Can I suggest that potentially God is waiting for you to open your heart to Him? Trust in Him enough to see this area of your life restored.

Embracing God's truth in every area of your life takes trust in Him no matter the outcome; being confident that He has our best interest at heart.

Fourthly, he embraced God's truth (v. 34b-35). When his sanity returned, he could have simply gone back to the way he was before. As I mentioned earlier, I don't see that happening due to the heart transformation. He could have also chosen to reject the truth about God, although it would not have been in his best interest. However, he decided to embrace that he was not the most powerful, the most honoured, and the earth's wisest. He gave that credit to God when he said, "No one can stop him or say to him "What do you mean by doing these things?"" (v. 35c). Is there a truth in your life to which God wants to open your eyes? Are you avoiding it, or are you learning to embrace it? Embracing God's truth in every area of your life takes trust in Him no matter the outcome; being confident that He has your best interest at heart.

For us to love others, we need to love ourselves. To love ourselves, we need Jesus' love.

Lastly, Nebuchadnezzar allowed love to flow into his heart. God has called us to be conduits for love. Jesus says one of the most important commands is to "love your neighbor as yourself. No other commandment is greater than these" (Mark 12:31). For us to love others, we need to love ourselves. To love ourselves, we need Jesus' love. Jesus is the one who teaches us how to love as "he first loved us" (1 John 4:19). It's encouraging that

Nebuchadnezzar's first response when his sanity came back was to worship. Of course, it was; he was grateful that God restored his mind. God first showed love to Nebuchadnezzar by coming to him in the wilderness, restoring his sanity, and ultimately restoring his kingdom. No wonder he wanted to worship God. Again, I ask you, are you letting love flow through your heart? Even those areas of your life that you wish no one to go near? Part of trusting God is allowing Him to deal with all the hurt, pain and shame in our hearts, allowing Him to flow into every nook and cranny until we are whole. Trusting God first comes from making a decision in our hearts that God is worth laying ourselves down in front of. He is worthy of knowing every intimate detail of our lives.

Journal one way that you can learn from King Nebuchadnezzar's journey to live a life of trust. How does this apply to your life?

JOURNAL

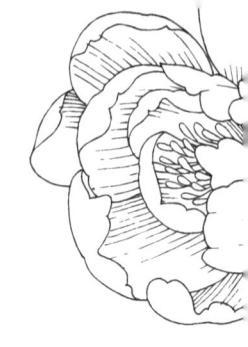

QUESTION

What are some ways that you can begin to get the Word of God in your heart?

"Store up treasures in heaven." Draw what this means to you.

DO
OD
LE
IT!

CHAPTER 6

Waiting Well

WHEN THE WAITING GETS LONG

Patience is not the ability to wait, but the ability to keep a good attitude while waiting. - Joyce Meyer

We all have to wait for something, whether that's a new job, a pay raise, a new house, a baby, a spouse. Waiting is not fun, especially when it begins to take longer than you anticipated. Waiting can drain you, and you can become weary when you have been waiting for God to fulfill a promise in your life. However, there is hope in the waiting, and there is a way that we can wait well until the promise arrives.

There was a woman in the Bible who knew all about waiting for a long time for her promise. Her name was Hannah. Hannah was married to Elkanah, who had two wives, herself and Peninnah.

Peninnah could have children, but Hannah couldn't. Each year, Elkanah would go to the Tabernacle to worship and sacrifice to the Lord. He would make sacrifices for each of his children and his wives. He loved both his wives very much. However, as much as he loved Hannah, he would only give one portion of meat for her sacrifice because she had no children. Peninnah would make fun of Hannah because the Lord did not give her children (1 Samuel 1:3-6).

Each year this would go on when Elkanah would go to the Tabernacle. Hannah would get so upset that she would be reduced to tears and not eat anything. She was experiencing deep hurt. One year, Hannah decided to go with Elkanah and pray at the Tabernacle. The Bible states that "Hannah was in deep anguish, crying bitterly as she prayed to the Lord." (1 Samuel 1:10). Hannah prayed this prayer of faith and trust:

> O Lord of Heaven's Armies, if you will look upon my sorrow and answer my prayer and give me a son, then I will give him back to you. He will be yours for his entire lifetime, and as a sign that he has been dedicated to the Lord, his hair will never be cut (1 Samuel 1:11, NLT).

Eli, the High Priest, sees her praying and thinks she is drunk as she is moving her lips, but no sound is coming out. He realizes she actually isn't drunk and ends up blessing her. The following year, Hannah was able to conceive a child with Elkanah (1 Samuel 1:20). God answered Hannah's prayer. But, what if you are still waiting on that promise from God like me? What happens then? I believe that this is where your trust in God is truly tested. Joyce Meyer says that waiting well is defined by keeping a good attitude during our seasons of waiting. To understand what this means, let's look at what attitude is. An attitude is "the way a person views something or tends to behave towards it; a position of the body indicating mood or emotion" [xxiii]. Our attitudes are our perspective and heart posture during the waiting periods.

> *Nobody likes to wait, but waiting will help you develop patience and deepens your trust in God. - Daree Allen*

Have you ever been waiting so long for something that when you pray to God, all that comes out is a whole lot of tears? I know I have. I have been on such an emotional roller coaster when waiting for my future spouse. I have been through doubting that he will ever come, to thinking I was ready and not thinking I was ready, to fearing that he will never come into my life. There were moments when my heart yearned for a spouse and a godly marriage, but it just didn't come. Some of those moments turned into despair and discouragement. Some of those moments lasted for just a moment, and others lasted for months and even years. In these moments of dark despair, I admit that I struggled to trust God and His plan for my life. I would think, "How can God just let me sit here and wait and yearn for something that he placed within my heart?" My heart broke as the years went by, and a spouse was nowhere to be found. That type of hurt doesn't just go away; you have to choose to trust God and process and work through the hurt to overcome it (Remember Chapter 1?).

My question to you is, what is your perspective during your waiting season? May I suggest that if you are in a place of dark despair and sadness, then you may need a perspective shift? God is an Almighty God; there is nothing too hard for Him. Instead of focusing on what you are waiting for, focus on what God is doing in your life right now. I am part of a Christian single's group on Facebook, where we encourage, advise and pray for each other. One day, someone posted a challenge to comment with one thing you are thankful for in this season of singleness. I absolutely loved this post because it shifted my perspective to what God was currently doing in my life and away from what I wanted Him to do in the future.

What is the posture of your heart as you are waiting? Is your heart set on what is to come and the potential out there? Are you fixated on what isn't in your life rather than focusing on what is? Are you focused on becoming the right person before you meet that right person? Hannah's heart posture was one of humility. She went and prayed, and although bitter tears came out of her, she knew she had to take it to God (1 Samuel 1:10). She knew that

God was the only one who could give her her heart's desires. Hannah fixed her heart on God's character (we talked about this in the first chapter).

Trusting God is a heart posture, a posture of laying down in front of Him, laying bare our whole life at His feet.

Trusting God is a heart posture, a posture of laying down in front of Him, laying bare our whole life at His feet. It wasn't until Hannah changed her heart posture that she got a new perspective on her situation. Hannah even decided to dedicate her baby to the Lord and be raised in the temple, if God blessed her with a child. We don't know why God didn't give her children until this point, but how do we know her season of desperation culminated in her trusting God enough to dedicate her unborn child to Him? To trust God, we need to change our heart posture. We need to shift our perspective on who God is. How can we change our heart posture to thrive in our seasons of waiting instead of barely surviving as Hannah did initially?

WHEN THE WAITING GETS TOUGH

Have you ever been in a season of waiting, where not only does it seem to drag on, but it's hard to withstand? It's a tough season of waiting for you. Job had a season like that in his life. Sure, you can look at Job and say it's hard to relate to him because you have never had everything taken away from you, including your health, in a moment. But how do you know that that is all it takes; one moment to change your life? Maybe it's a bad diagnosis, a death in the family, or being laid off at work? Whatever it is, it's hard to endure those seasons sometimes.

Job had it all, ten children - seven of them were boys, a wife who loved him, thousands of livestock (back then, that was their currency), and many servants to take care of all of that. The Bible says he was "the richest person in that entire area" (Job 1:3). Then one day, Satan came to God to challenge Job's dedication to Him. He contested that Job only feared God because God protected him and made him rich. So God allowed Satan to "do whatever" he wanted "with everything he possesses." (Job 1:12). Slowly, but surely Satan took away Job's children, his livestock and then his servants. Most of his livelihood was gone.

That did not satisfy Satan. He decided to take it one step further and take away Job's health - "he struck Job with terrible boils from head to foot" (Job 2:7). So let's put this in a context that we can understand today. Let's pretend you're Job, and you have lots of children, a great marriage, lots of money in the bank, you own multiple properties, and you own a business and have many employees. By definition, you are rich. All of a sudden, your children are killed in a freak accident. The bank you have money with loses your money. A freak storm simultaneously destroys your properties. And someone embezzles money from your business, leaving you having to close it down and fire all your employees. How would you feel?

On top of it all, Job's friends come and try to console him in his pain and grief. When they first arrive, they are truly sincere in their efforts. They weep and wail with him, tear their robes and throw dust over their heads to show their grief. They sit there with him in silence for seven days and seven nights (Job 2:11-13). Then Job speaks out his grief. After he does so, Eliphaz decides to speak. What happens next is they each take turns figuratively kicking Job while he's down with their words. They mock him and blame him for what happened in his life. One even tells Job that it's time to get over his loss. How would you feel if you were going through it, and instead of coming and consoling, I decided to condemn you? I'm sure they were well-meaning and looking out for Job's interests by ensuring he didn't sin in his grief. However, they caused more ill than good will.

Bible scholars have guessed that Job went through this season of loss for anywhere from two to four years, but they can't be sure, and the Bible isn't clear on this. All we do know is that he went through an immense trial. If I were in Job's shoes, giving up would have looked like a real good option. But, guess what? Job didn't give up! Yes, he was at his lowest, and he was grieving some pretty significant losses in his life.

He lost his children, his livestock, his servants, his farmhands, and his health. Satan struck Job with terrible boils from head to toe. So much so that he had to use broken shards of pottery to scrape them off of his skin (Job 2: 8). Despite all this, he remained faithful. As much as he misspoke against God in his anguish, he still chose to speak to God.

I believe Job's heart was in the right place throughout his whole season of grief. As he waited for God to deliver him from his circumstances, he may have said things that maybe he shouldn't have. However, he showed us what trusting God looked like in these types of seasons. Firstly, when Satan took away all his livestock, children and servants, his first response was to fall to the ground and worship God (Job 1:20). Job didn't blame God (v. 22); he didn't roll around on the floor and say, "Why me?" Instead, he dropped to his knees and humbled himself before the Master.

Secondly, when Satan struck Job with boils, his wife advised him that he should curse God so that He would strike him and he would die. He replied to her saying, "You talk like a foolish woman. Should we accept only good things from the hand of God and never anything bad?" (Job 2:10). When his wife corrected him, he reminded her of the character of God. Job knew the character of God, and even during his significant loss, he chose to trust in God's character.

Lastly, Job finally repented when God challenged him in what he said. In Job 42:2, Job said to God, "I know that you can do anything, and no one can stop you." You asked, 'Who is this that questions my wisdom with such ignorance?' It is I - and I was talking about things I knew nothing about, things far too wonderful for me." (NLT). Right here, Job admitted his shortcomings before God. He went on to say in verse 6: "I take back everything I said, and I sit in dust and ashes to show my repentance." In his grief, pain, and season of wait, he repented to God. Job showed God in his actions that He trusted Him; He trusted His plans. The mere gesture of sitting down in dust and ashes can be seen as a physical sign of laying down all his own knowledge and wisdom at God's feet. That is trust. Shortly after that, God used Job to pray on behalf of his friends to forgive their sins.

God then restored his fortunes to double what he lost.

I believe that there was a heart change within Job when he decided to sit down in the dust and ashes. It was this heart change that opened the door to his blessing. This is an excellent example of how it unlocks the blessings in our lives when we trust God.

How many of us want to stop following God when we go through challenging situations that last a long time? Do we want to throw in the towel to this whole "Christian thing?" I can honestly say that my first response would be to throw a pity party for one and ask, "Why me?" and "What did I do to deserve this?" I would focus on the lack. I would want to hide away in a cave somewhere until everyone forgot who I was. I would want to move and start over. I have been there. Remaining faithful isn't easy, and it takes trusting God even when things are hard.

A few years ago, shortly after I started working for my church as the Kids Ministry Director, God brought me through a season of testing. It was an intense season of character building. When God wants to shape your character, he will put you through a series of events, situations and circumstances to apply the right amount of pressure to help you change. God called me to work for people. I was excited at first, but six

To stay faithful in a difficult situation takes a level of

trust

in God that He will turn it all around for your good.

months in, I was thrown for a loop after my first complaint from a parent. I'm just going to say it: people are complicated. During this season, I learned patience, grace, mercy, how to truly love others in the face of adversity. What made it so hard for me was that it was unexpected. I learned to do hard things. Before, I would have just given up and walked away. I called those years the wilderness years. God used those years to shape and mould me.

When God shapes us, He must use pressure. I felt stuck so many times through this season. I felt the weight of the season. More times than I would like to admit, I was ready to throw in the towel. I wanted to quit my job and give up. I would run to God with tear-streaked cheeks throughout this season and ask Him, "Why?" "What are you doing in me?" He would answer, in the way God does - in that still small voice, "Remain faithful." I would get so upset with Him because I wanted to give up and quit. But he wouldn't let me. In those moments, my trust in God was what got me through.

When I was having one of those moments, God gave me this Scripture in Luke 16:10, which says, "if you are faithful in little things, you will be faithful in large ones." God wanted me to remain faithful in this season so that He could bless me with the much he had planned for my life. To stay faithful in a difficult situation takes a level of trust in God that He will turn it all around for your good. I had to trust God that He knew what he was doing with my life and that if He needed me in my position at the church, then that's where I needed to be.

I don't know what difficult season you are going through right now. Trust God that He knows what He is doing in your life, even if it seems longer than expected. Let's take a page out of Job's life and learn to worship God through it, remember His character and repent of any sin that we need to. I believe that we will be on the other side of this saying; it was worth the wait.

WHEN YOU'RE DONE WITH WAITING

> *Trusting Him to work out your circumstances instead of using your own might and power will bring deep satisfying joy into your life.* – Joyce Meyer

Have you ever been to that point in your season of waiting when you're just done? Or you're ready to make something happen in your own strength and just walk away from it all?

Throughout the Bible, we see men and women who waited, some well and some not so well. Jesus waited thirty years to start his ministry, and his mother, Mary, waited thirty years and nine months to see the promise of redemption for her people fulfilled through the ministry of her son. Joseph waited twenty-seven years to see his dreams become a reality, and Jacob waited seven years for Rebekah. Also, the Israelites - God's own people, waited over forty years to enter the Promised Land.

Many times, while the Israelites were waiting to enter the Promised Land, they wanted to give up. The Bible comments on three different times they complained about their situation. One of these times, they had just arrived in the wilderness of Zin, for the third time, to a place called Kadesh (Numbers 20:1). It was no Promised Land. Their first response was to blame Moses and Aaron. They said in verses 3-5,

> If only we had died in the Lord's presence with our brothers! Why have you brought the congregation of the Lord's people into this wilderness to die, along with all our livestock? Why did you make us leave Egypt and bring us here to this terrible place? This land has no grain, no figs, no grapes, no pomegranates and no water to drink! (NLT)

The way that God led them through the wilderness- fire at night and a pillar of cloud by day - took them in circles for years. They literally were going around the same mountain over and over, and at the first hint of hardship or difference, they were ready to walk away.

In Numbers 12, we see Moses' own siblings turn against him. Miriam and Aaron complained that Moses married a Cushite woman and questioned if God only spoke to Moses and no one else. As a result, Miriam was struck with leprosy and removed from camp for seven days. The story continued in Numbers 13 when Moses sent twelve men (one from each tribe of Israel) to scout the Promised Land and assess its viability. They all came back with a good report about the vegetation and produce within the land. However, all except two warned the Israelites that their enemies were too powerful and dissuaded the people from taking the land (Numbers 13). So the Israelites complained against Moses, Aaron and the Lord. God punished them by not allowing anyone who was twenty years of age or older and was included in the Registration (the first census taken of the people once they crossed the Red Sea) to enter the Promised Land (Numbers 14). Basically, anyone who was there when God first spoke to the Israelites about the Promised Land. Here we see the Israelites in Kadesh, a land not flowing with milk and honey. The only people they had to blame for that were themselves. They were the ones who complained to God about their circumstances. They gave up.

I understand that the wilderness is not a comfortable place to be. It's a place where God moulds us and shapes us. The wilderness is not meant to be pleasant. It could be hard to continue waiting when you have been waiting as long as the Israelites had been. Suffice to say, they were done with waiting.

When I first came to Christ, I lived in England, and God told me that it was time to go back to Canada. My first response was to ask Him, "What am I going to do in Canada?" My life had been in England for almost five years, and even though at that moment I was jobless, I didn't want to go back to Canada to be unemployed and living in my parent's house. I heard God say to me so clearly that I was going to lead Children's Ministry, lead kids in worship, teach them to love Jesus and that I was going to be an administrator. My life was closed within two weeks, and I was on a plane back to Canada. A month later, I got a job in a hospital - not working with kids. At the time, I lived with my parents, which was not ideal for me after living independently for five years.

At this point, I was attending a church that was really far away from me. I didn't have my own car, so I had to rely on my dad's car or get a ride from someone. I stopped attending that church because of the distance. So, I was now churchless but I knew I was meant to lead hospital as a medical secretary - nowhere near what God had called me to do. The following year I begin to serve in the Children's ministry at our church. It was right around when I learned about the internship our church had offered. Yes, it was for younger adults and older teens, and I was in my 30's, but I knew I had to take it. Our church's internship offered college bible classes along with firsthand experience in how a church runs from day to day.

A year later, I did our church's internship while working for our local University. I was on a contract with them, and it was coming to an end at the same time my internship was winding down. It was the last week of the internship, and one of our pastors approached me to offer me a job at the church. I know what you're thinking, "Wow, you finally got there!" Yes, I was a step closer to stepping into the specific will God had called me to, but I wasn't there yet. I want to note that I had completely forgotten about the word God had spoken to me at this point.

Fast forward two years later, and an opportunity arises for me to oversee our Children's ministry. It is interesting how it worked out. God said that I would be an administrator for the Children's Ministry. The Children's Pastor was transitioning to become our Lead Pastor, which they are now. So, when my bosses approached me, they offered me the position to become the Children's Ministry Administrator or the LH Kids Director - to be more specific. That was a total of six years in the making. I had waited all those years to see God's promise fulfilled in my life.

To say that I was over waiting during those six years is an understatement. I went on another emotional roller coaster, from being nowhere close to that promise to getting hired at the church, only to do a completely different job. To then, finally being offered the job that fulfilled the promise. I wasn't looking forward to the future while staying present in the present. I wanted to be in that "Promised Land job" now. When working at our local University, I remember being so discouraged. I had no idea, a year later, I would be working for the church and getting closer to my promise.

> *Waiting well looks forward to the future while staying present in the present. Waiting well means I remain open to God and allow Him to move me toward the future he has planned in his time. - Wendy Pope*

Yes, it's easy to give up on our dreams when they take longer to come to pass. May I suggest that while you're waiting, you press into God? Wendy Pope says in her quote above that waiting well looks like remaining open to God to move us toward our future. Can we be people who allow God to do what He needs to do in us, through us and to us, to get closer to our Promised Land? Will we trust God enough, lay down our lives in front of Him, including the object of our wait, to allow Him to move us toward our Promised Land? I believe that's how we overcome the negative thought cycle of being done with waiting. Maybe this perspective shift will allow us to thrive in this season until we receive our promise.

WHEN TRUST IS THE ONLY ANSWER

Have you ever felt like you were in an impossible situation and you just had no way out? You felt like you were stuck between a rock and a hard place? It is where Mary was. Let's look at the book of Luke, chapter one, verse twenty-six, where an angel visits Mary. At this point, Mary has lived a holy life. She is a virgin and is engaged to Joseph, a local carpenter. The angel tells Mary in verses 31-33,

> You will conceive and give birth to a son, and you will name him Jesus. He will be very great and will be called the Son of the Most High. The Lord God will give him the throne of his ancestor David. And he will reign over Israel forever; his Kingdom will never end!

Got Questions, a website dedicated to answering your biblical questions, cites that "Jewish marriage customs regarding a couple's engagement were far different and much more stringent... Marriages were arranged by the parents of the bride and groom and often without even consulting the couple to be married. A contract was prepared in which the groom's parents paid a bride price. Such a contract was immediately deemed binding, with the couple considered married even though the actual ceremony and consummation of the marriage would not occur for as long as a year afterwards" [xxiv]. If this happened to Mary, it would be scandalous. It was known to both sets of parents that Joseph and Mary had not consummated their marriage as they hadn't had the ceremony yet. To do that before marriage was considered a big no-no.

Mary's response to the angel wasn't to laugh at him or start trying to figure out in her mind how she could make it happen in her own strength. No instead, she asked him how it would happen. After he explained to her that it would happen through the power of the Holy Spirit (v. 34), she said to him in verse 38, "I am the Lord's servant. May everything you have said about me come true." She trusted God that He would take care of every detail. Even the most complicated ones to come.

Fast-forward to the birth. After Mary gives birth to Jesus, shepherds come and visit them. The shepherds tell Mary and Joseph everything the angels told him, "I bring you good news that will bring great joy to all people. The Saviour - yes, the Messiah, the Lord- has been born today in Bethlehem, the city of David. And you will recognize him by this sign: You will find a baby wrapped snugly in strips of cloth, lying in a manger" (Luke 2:10-12). By now, if there was any doubt in Mary's heart about who her son is, there isn't anymore. It says in verse 38 "...but Mary kept all these things in her heart and thought about them often."

Mary had to wait. First, she is visited by an angel and then the shepherds come and repeat what the angel told her. She had to wait to see the promise over Jesus' life fulfilled. Can you imagine being the mother of Jesus? Knowing that your son is the great Messiah your people have been waiting for, for thousands of years? And yet, she kept all these things in her heart. I believe that her trust in God allowed her to keep these things to herself while she waited. What else could she do? She couldn't even try to make any of this happen in her own strength. It sounded so preposterous and impossible that it was only by the hand of God that it could happen. Yet, she chose to wait. Let me note that Mary didn't just sit down and wait for Jesus to grow up and become the great King of Kings. Mary still had to take care of Him, wean Him and feed Him. She had to raise Him. I'm sure God spoke to Mary on how to discipline Him and shape Him in this season.

There was another time when Mary got a glimpse of what Jesus' public ministry would look like. They were on the way back home from Jerusalem, and they misplaced Jesus. When they realized He was missing three days later, they found Him in the temple preaching the word of God (Luke 2:41-51).

God likes to help those who are already helping themselves.

Sometimes, we feel that we need to be passive in our seasons of wait. However, the opposite is true. God calls us to take action in the seasons of wait. God likes to help those who are already helping themselves. He calls us to do what we can until the wait is over.

If you feel like you are in a situation where you have no other choice but to wait on God, figure out what He wants you to do and start doing it.

If you feel like you are in a situation where you have no other choice but to wait on God, figure out what He wants you to do and start doing it.

Doing something while you wait shows God that you trust Him to work it all out for your good.

I used to own a 2001 Toyota Corolla. It was silver with automatic windows and a CD player. For a car that old, it was luxury. I named it JJ (a reminder of Jehovah Jireh, which means God is Provider) because God provided for this car. Slowly but surely, things started to break down in my vehicle. First, the automatic windows began to stick in the middle of winter. I remember one cold, snowy morning, pressing the button to roll down my window so I could clean the rear-view mirror. When I was done, I pressed the button to wind it back up, and it wouldn't come up. It was stuck! It wasn't until I was driving a few minutes in the freezing cold of the morning; I tried it again, and it finally came back up. Secondly, I had fixed the exhaust on that car six or more times. A clue that the car was a lemon would have been when the exhaust fell off my car while driving it one day on my way to work. Suffice to say, that car was a dud.

The time finally came when I had to let go of my car. As much as the car was starting to fall apart, it was still sudden and unexpected. I was hoping it would last at least another year. My insurance was going to go up by $100 per month. So, like any good financial steward,

I looked into other insurance options. I found a much cheaper one. However, they said that I would need to get it safetied to insure it. A part of me knew that my car wouldn't pass the safety test but I got a mechanic to look at it anyway. Basically, there was a massive hole in the bottom of my car, the muffler was on the way out, and the brakes needed replacing. That was the end of old JJ.

At this point, I had no money saved up to buy a new car because all my money went into fixing the vehicle. I was in a place where I had no other choice but to trust God. My first response was to cry. After I cried, I sat down, and I prayed. I talked to God about what happened like God didn't know, and I made my requests known to God.

Part of trusting God is learning not to worry. Philippians 4:6 says, "don't worry about anything; instead pray about everything. Tell God what you need, and thank him for all he has done" (NLT). Matthew 6:31 also says, "So don't worry about these things, saying 'What will we eat? What will we drink? What will we wear?' These things dominate the thoughts of unbelievers, but your heavenly Father already knows all your needs" (NLT). Before we take our needs or before that need comes up, we must understand that God already knows about them. He also knows how He is going to provide for that need. He knows all (omniscient). We have to learn to trust Him to work it out.

A week after discovering that I needed to buy a new car, someone came to me and gave me a cheque for $6000. Yes, you read that correctly. It's unheard of, right? Well, not in God's economy. God came through just like what it says in His Word: "And this same God who takes care of me will supply all your needs from his glorious riches, which have been given to us in Christ Jesus" (Philippians 4:19, NLT).

A season of six long months followed where I searched for my new car. I have never had that much money before to buy a vehicle, so I wanted to take my time making the right choice. No car equals taking the bus and Ubers everywhere. I made it work, but I never want to return to that season again. It was hard. I needed a car for my job, and I didn't have one. During that time, our church opened a second campus. As the LH Kids Director, I was responsible for getting all the kid's classrooms furnished. I look back and think how I did that, but God always came through. Finally, on December 31, I picked up "Midnight Blue," my 2006 Honda Civic. This car is such a blessing to me, and I appreciate it so much more, having gone through my season of lack.

Our trust unlocks God's power in our lives.

I believe that God places us in impossible situations to remind us that He is still in control. They also teach us to rely on God and not our own strength. There is a reason why the Bible says, "what is impossible with man is possible with God" (Luke 18:2, NIV). God wants us to trust Him so He can work in our lives. Our trust unlocks God's power in our lives. During the week before I received that cheque, I was determined to trust God in this area of my life, no matter what. He is the Jehovah Jireh, He provides, and loves blessing His children. If you find yourself in a situation where you have no other choice but to trust God, always choose to trust God. You'll be thankful you did.

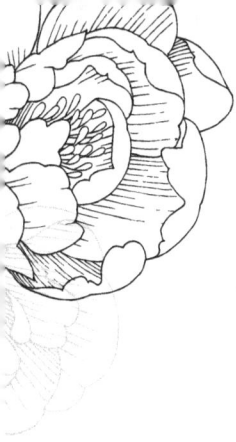

Journal about a time in your life you had to wait for a long time for something. What was your perspective in that season?

JOUR
NAL

DOODLE IT!

Draw a picture of you receiving the promises you are waiting on God for.

QUESTION

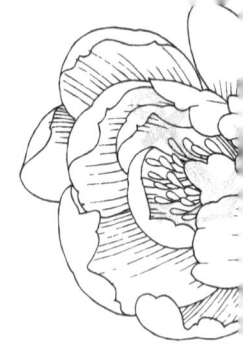

Have you ever been in a situation where you wanted to give up? How did you remain faithful?

_____
_____
_____
_____
_____
_____
_____
_____
_____
_____
_____

CHAPTER 7

Keep Your Eyes Up!

JESUS- THE ONLY WAY!

Isaiah 43:2 says, "When you go through deep waters, I will be with you, when you go through rivers of difficulty, you will not drown..." Remember the Old Testament definition of trust: "to lie extended on the ground"? When you are lying down extended, you need to look up to see anything. That's what trust is. Trust is looking up at Jesus at all times. Trust believes that He is always with us, even when the waters get deep. He promises that we will not drown. The only way not to drown is to keep our eyes on Jesus. The only way to remember that God is with us is if we keep our eyes on Him.

The more you trust Jesus and keep your eyes focused on Him, the more life you'll have. - Joyce Meyer

I spoke earlier about the wilderness season I was in. As we learned before, the wilderness seasons are there to shape and mould us. They are supposed to be hard. A diamond can never be a diamond if other rocks around it don't apply pressure. It's under the pressure of surrounding rocks that a diamond is formed. TD Jakes says, "The bigger the anointing, the bigger the crushing." It basically means that if you are experiencing a lot of pressure in your life, in the season you are in, to be exact, then it's most likely because God wants to use you in a big way.

The pressure in my wilderness season was real; it was overwhelming. Some of it was self-induced - the pressure to be perfect, to not make mistakes, to know how to do everything, and to do it all. But it was also external. The pressure of others to get it right all the time, and do it a certain way. I found this season difficult and wanted to give up many times. I remember one time when I was ready to throw in the towel. I don't think it was one specific thing that put me over the edge, but I was done. I wanted to walk away from life, every single aspect of it. That morning God gave me a revelation in this season. I felt like I was drowning in this season like I couldn't keep my head above water.

Then the song Oceans by Hillsong began to play on my morning devotional playlist, and God gave me a vision. He gave me a vision of me walking into an ocean from the shore. In this vision, He asked me to continue going into the water. The further I went, the deeper the water got. Then He asked me where I was looking. I said, "Up." He told me that's where I was right now. I was in deep waters, and instead of looking around me or down, I needed to be looking up at Him. He said the deeper you go into the water; you are forced to look up. He said that I needed to keep my eyes on the source during this season, or I would drown.

That broke and put me back together all at the same time. I needed to hear that. I needed to be reminded that I wasn't alone in this season, that this season wasn't going to break me. I came out of that moment, ready to tackle my life. That revelation sustained me, and it's a memory I often recall when I feel like life is just a bit too much to handle.

In the Bible, we meet a man named Peter who loved Jesus so much. There was a moment when Peter had to decide whether to follow Jesus or go his own way. Jesus had just finished teaching about how He was the Bread of Life and that those who eat this bread from heaven would have eternal life (John 6:53). Jesus goes on to say, "But anyone who eats my flesh and drinks my blood has eternal life, and I will raise that person at the last day" (John 6:54). Of course, Jesus was not saying that if people literally ate His flesh and drank His blood, He would give them eternal life. He's not a vampire (Lol). No, He was saying that if they had faith in Jesus that He was the Son of God, that He would give them eternal life. A lot of people struggled with the concept that He was preaching. John 6:66 says, "At this point, many of his disciples turned away and deserted him."

The thing with truth is that when you hear it, you want more of it. Lies will no longer do.

Jesus goes on to ask the twelve disciples, "Are you also going to leave?" Peter replies, "Lord, to whom would we go? You have the words that give eternal life. We believe, and we know you are the Holy One of God" (John 6:67-69, NLT). You see, the disciples lived and worked in the world. They knew all about that. However, everything changed when they decided to follow Jesus. They were spiritually blind, and He opened their eyes. Jesus spoke words of wisdom. He answered questions they had about God and Scripture. He told the truth. The thing with truth is that when you hear it, you want more of it. Lies will no longer do.

There was no way they could go back to their old lives. That's why Peter said, "to whom would we go?" He knew that there was no one else like Jesus on the earth. Jesus radically changed his life, so why would he go anywhere else - he couldn't go anywhere else. That's where I was in that wilderness season of my life. I already lived a life that was of the world; then, I met Jesus. I didn't want to go back to my other life, so I had no other choice in that season but to continue keeping my eyes on Jesus. Only Jesus had the life-giving words that would fuel me, inspire me, set me free; during this season. I had to be confident that

When our eyes are *focused* on Jesus, the next thing we know, we have accomplished the very thing we were running from.

when my eyes were on Him that He would be able to get me through any difficult situation.

Are you in a challenging situation in your life where you know you can't go back to the way things were, but moving forward looks daunting? Maybe God is asking you to move to a new country, take on a new job, write that book, learn a new skill, love the unlovable, reach the unreached, go on that long-term missions trip? Or maybe God is calling you to face that trauma, overcome those habits and lifestyle choices that have been hindering your growth? Wherever you are in life, take the stand today to always choose Jesus. You will never regret that choice. I'm so glad that I did because I have seen Him come through in my life, time and time again. It is how we show we trust Him while keeping our eyes on Him. When our eyes are focused on Jesus, the next thing we know, we have accomplished the very thing we were running from.

WATERS RUN DEEP

Once, I saw this quote: "Trust Jesus enough to let things happen." I don't know who said it, but I like it. Do you trust Jesus enough to allow things to happen in your life? Allow things to fall into place? I don't know about you, but this goes against every part of my being. God created me to be a planner through and through. I love planning. I always say that I started the "dream big" phrase (not actually), as I have dreamed big since I was a little girl. I love dreaming big dreams and then making plans to see them come to fruition. I like knowing where I am going.

Before I said yes to Jesus, I was an avid goal-setter, and I liked everything in my life planned out. I left little room for spontaneity. Then I met Jesus, and He turned my life upside down. I was living in England at the time, and I thought I would stay there. I had finished my Master's degree in Theatre Directing and thought for sure that I would be a famous theatre director somewhere in London, England. Instead, God sent me back home to Hamilton, Ontario, Canada. That was not the first time that He would interrupt my life. As I mentioned before, I currently work for my church, overseeing our Children's Ministry.

You see, the thing with plans is that we are supposed to make them, but then we are supposed to surrender them all to God. King Solomon, who is famous for asking God to gift him with wisdom, says it ideally, "Within your heart you can make plans for your future, but the Lord chooses the steps you take to get there" (Proverbs 16:9, TPT). It takes trust to make plans that you are excited about stepping into, achieving or crushing, but then having to surrender it all to God. What has given me comfort in this area of my life is summed up nicely in this Scripture: "Before you do anything, put your trust totally in God and not in yourself. Then every plan you make will succeed" (Proverbs 16:3, TPT). This Scripture made me rethink how I define success. My pastor once asked me the question, "What is success to you?" Because of the context with which this question was asked, I was confident that success is accomplishing God's will for you here on earth.

Psalms 139:16 says, "You saw me before I was born. Every day of my life was recorded in your book. Every moment was laid out before a single day has passed." God knew what would happen in your life before you were even born. He recorded every day and moment in His book, all laid out before. God is the ultimate planner, so remember this when He asks us to trust Him with our plans. God wants the best for you. He has plans to give you a future and a hope (Jeremiah 29:11).

So how do we keep our eyes on Jesus when our plans go sideways? Jesus' disciples know all about their plans going sideways. In Matthew 14, we read about how Jesus feeds the 5000 (Matthew 14: 21). Right after that, He sends His disciples across the other side of the lake by boat. While out on the water, they encountered a big storm and "were fighting heavy waves" (v.24). Before this, Jesus was up on the hill talking to God by himself. The Bible says, "About three o'clock in the morning. Jesus came toward them, walking on water" (Matthew 14: 25).

The body of water that Jesus walked on was not just any body of water. It was a sea, the Sea of Galilee, to be exact. "The lake has a surface area of 64 square miles (166 square km). Its maximum depth, measured in the northeast, is 157 feet (48 metres). Extending 13 miles (21 km) from north to south and 7 miles (11 km) from east to west, it is pear-shaped" [xxv]. The Sea of Galilee was one of the largest freshwater sources in the area, flowing down into the Jordan River and finally into the Dead Sea. It was a popular destination for the vibrant fishing industry during the New Testament. "Its semi-tropical climate combined with the sulphur springs in Tiberias made the Sea of Galilee a popular health resort destination for sick people" [xxvi]. Scholars believe that Jesus may have targeted the area because of the number of sick people drawn to it. Many important events in Jesus' life took place around this Sea, including the calling of the disciples; Peter, Andrew, James and John. Jesus called Matthew to ministry in Capernaum, which borders the Sea of Galilee. This body of water was significant.

In Matthew 14:28, we pick up our story with Peter saying to Jesus, "Lord, if it's really you, tell me to come to you, walking on the water." Jesus tells Peter to come. We all remember how the story goes; Peter starts to walk on water towards Jesus. But then something happens that derails him. "But when he saw the strong wind and the waves, he was terrified and began to sink" (Matthew 14:30). I can just imagine the scene, the waves are going, and the winds are strong, but as he sees Jesus walk on water, Peter thinks with all the faith in his heart that he can do it too. I mean, he just saw Jesus feed the 5000; why couldn't he do this? He gets off the boat, entirely focused on Jesus and then starts to walk on water, but quickly the elements around him distract him, and his fear begins to sink him.

If we look at the version in Mark, the Bible says that Jesus saw that the disciples were in serious trouble and came to them walking on water. It also says that He intended to pass them (Mark 6:48). The Gospel of John says that the disciples were on the shore waiting for Jesus. When Jesus didn't show up, they decided to go across the Lake to Capernaum by themselves. While on the water, they encountered a storm. During that storm, they saw Jesus coming to them, walking on water (John 6:16-21). No matter how events transpired in each version, they all end with Jesus assuring the disciples not to be afraid.

The thing with fear is that it can either propel you or sink you.

He uses the exact same words in each Gospel: "Don't be afraid. I am here!" (Matthew 14:27, Mark 6:50, John 6:20). The thing with fear is that it can either propel you or sink you. In the case of Peter, he got to be part of one of the most noted miracles that Jesus performed. So how can we learn to keep our eyes on Jesus in the presence of the unknown? Peter was a fisherman. It was on the shore of Galilee where he spent his life. He must have known the waters pretty well and faced a fierce storm or two during this time. What was it about this storm that sank him? I believe it was his focus. You see, when we are in the storms of our lives, our eyes must stay focused on Jesus. As soon as we take them off, we begin to be carried by the waves of doubt, fear and the unknown. What if's start to circle in our mind, and if we are not careful, we could begin to take matters into our own hands.

By focusing on Jesus, we surrender our limitations to Him and allow Him to bring us through.

Remember, Peter saw the winds and the waves (Matthew 14: 30). It didn't say he felt them. He saw the force of the winds with his own eyes. However, he must have felt it too. Was the water not slapping against his face? Did the wind not almost knock him over? I'm sure it did, but I'm also sure that he was used to that feeling. So why didn't that prevent him from getting out of the boat? He knew what it felt like to be tossed by the waves; it was almost second nature to him. He was a fisherman, after all. What happened when he chose to focus on the force of the winds? He became terrified and began to sink. We see right here why focusing on Jesus in our storms is how we show we trust Him. We choose to look up to Jesus, who can bring us through any storm. By focusing on Jesus, we surrender our limitations to Him and allow Him to bring us through.

We are currently in the middle of a global pandemic in our world, and at the time of writing this book, my city is in our third lockdown. It means that we cannot meet with others in their homes, go to the mall without getting screened and standing in a line, and we cannot even meet with a group of friends of more than five people. We have been on and off like this for the last thirteen months. The pandemic has been a long season for the whole world. Since our first lockdown, I believe we have come a long way, where no one could go anywhere. The virus was unknown, and people lived in fear. They still do today.

Keeping my eyes on Jesus, I have learned to thrive in a season where others were just surviving, barely getting by.

Only one thing has gotten me through this season: that is Jesus. Keeping my eyes on Jesus, I have learned to thrive in a season where others were just surviving, barely getting by. I learned to keep my eyes on Him concerning my finances when others were losing their jobs. I learned to press in and receive healing and gained a new perspective where I struggled before. All of this was only possible by keeping my eyes on Jesus. It could have been easy to allow a global pandemic, the threat of being potentially laid off, to take my focus. But I didn't let it. Denise Campbell Mays says, "Keep your eyes fixed on God. The moment you look elsewhere, therein awaits a wealth of confusion." Our confusion comes from us taking matters into our own hands by focusing on our problems. When we focus on our issues, we become problem solvers and inherently become overwhelmed because of the size of our problems. We were never meant to solve our own problems; God didn't create us to carry that weight. That's why we have Jesus. If you are in deep waters today, choose to trust Jesus by keeping your eyes on Him; He will rescue you and bring you to safety.

NOWHERE TO TURN

David had an uncanny way of keeping his eyes on God no matter what he was going through. Right after David is anointed the next king of Israel, God sends Saul a tormenting spirit. One of his servants tells him about David, who can play the harp, hoping to soothe him. Saul sends for David to come live with him. Saul ends up loving David like one of his sons, and he becomes his armour-bearer (1 Samuel 16:14-22).

Now David was living in the palace with Saul but going home to help his ageing father take care of the sheep. As stated previously, David's dad sends him to his brothers, who were fighting the Philistines, and he kills Goliath. Soon after his defeat, Saul becomes jealous of David's success and begins to make attempts on his life. David is then forced to go on the run for his life while King Saul sends his greatest warriors to hunt him down and kill him. He was in constant danger and couldn't trust anyone. He was forced to hide in caves and out in the wilderness, away from civilization. He couldn't even see his family.

He finally returns to Judah after he learns about the death of King Saul. Once Saul dies, David is made king only of Judah, not all of Israel yet. That's because one of Saul's men took his son to Manahaim to proclaim him king over "Gilead, Jezreel, Ephraim, Benjamin...and the rest of Israel" (2 Samuel 2:9). Only when King Ishbosheth and his men end up murdering each other, David finally becomes king of all of Israel. Once he is king, he has many victories as he continues to acquire the Promised Land. Then his son Amnon rapes his half-sister Tamar. When Absalom, David's third son and Tamar's full brother, finds out, he kills his half-brother Amnon. Then Absalom turns on his father and conspires with Israel to harm King David. David is then forced to flee into the wilderness, this time from his own son.

David went through a lot and was on the run for his life twice. Not many people are on the run for their life even once. If David wanted to walk away from God, no one could blame him. If David was overwhelmed by his circumstances, no one could say a word. But David did something different. When he was on the run from Saul, he wrote these words: "I will thank the Lord because he is just; I will sing praise to the name of the Lord Most High" (Psalm 7:17). Even when he is scared for his life, David thanks God; he praises His name.

When David is advised to flee into the mountains because he isn't safe where he is, he writes these words: "But the Lord is in his holy Temple; the Lord still rules from heaven, He watches everyone closely, examining every person on earth" (Psalm 11:4). He declares that

I could just imagine what David's men who were with him on the run felt. They must have been terrified, doubted if God existed, and were just plain weary from constantly running. David was weary from always being on the run, but he never took his eyes off God. He knew the character of God as provider, all-powerful, lover, helper and Saviour. David trusted God and laid his heart before Him in every situation he found himself. He wrote these words while in the wilderness: "O God, you are my God; I earnestly search for you. My soul thirsts for you; my whole body longs for you in this parched and weary land where there is no water" (Psalm 63:1). He understood that it was better to look up rather than around him. In the wilderness, he had nowhere to turn but up. David recognized that it was better to place his trust in the Lord of Heaven's Armies than his circumstances.

Amid Saul hunting down David and his men, David writes Psalm 31. It says,

> Have mercy on me, Lord, for I am in distress. Tears blur my eyes. My body and soul are withering away. I am dying from grief; my years are shortened by sadness. Sin has drained my strength; I am wasting away from within. I am scorned by all my enemies and despised by my neighbors- even my friends are afraid to come near me. When they see me on the street, they run the other way. I am ignored as if I

were dead, as if I were a broken pot. I heard the many rumors about me, and I am surrounded by terror. My enemies conspired against me, plotting to take my life. But I am trusting you, O Lord, saying, "You are my God!" My future is in your hands. Rescue me from those who hunt me down relentlessly (Psalm 31:9-15, NLT).

We need to get to a point where we say that we choose to trust God no matter what is happening in our lives.

This is weariness; this is exhaustion. David had nowhere to turn; he couldn't trust anyone, including his friends. When we are in that moment in our lives, where we feel we have nowhere to turn, that's when we need to turn to Jesus. Our gaze needs to realign to Him. He is the source of our hope, joy, comfort, and strength. Jesus helps us get through any situation. "But I am trusting you, O Lord." We need to get to a point where we say that we choose to trust God no matter what is happening in our lives. We choose to keep our eyes focused on Jesus. That's how we trust Him.

Living by faith means listening to Jesus and choosing to trust him moment by moment. - Matt Eachus

Would you say that you trust Jesus moment by moment? It can be hard to trust Jesus in every circumstance. But Matt encourages us here that we live by faith by choosing to trust Jesus like this. Is there a trying situation in your life that you are going through right now? Maybe you have been going through a lengthy trial with your family, or a friend, or at work? Do you feel like it is just dragging on? Do you feel like you can't trust anyone around you and you have nowhere to turn? Jesus is waiting for you to look up so that He can help you. You won't regret that you did.

_____
_____
_____
_____
_____
_____
_____
_____
_____
_____
_____
_____
_____
_____

JOURNAL

Journal about this quote: "Living by faith means listening to Jesus and choosing to trust him moment by moment."

DOODLE IT!

Draw some of the BIG dreams you have for your life.

QUESTION

Do you set goals? Why or why not?

CHAPTER 8

His Will, Not Mine

THE THREE WILLS OF GOD

Many words throughout the Bible are used to describe God's will. To understand what it means to say 'His will, not mine', we should understand what exactly God's will is. For the purposes of this chapter, let's look at how the word "will" is used in Romans 12:2: "Don't copy the behaviour and customs of this world, but let God transform you into a new person by changing the way you think. Then you will learn to know God's will for you, which is good and pleasing and perfect." The Greek word for will in this Scripture is thelema which properly means "God's preferred-will; His best offer to people which can be accepted or rejected" [xxvii].

In Discerning God's Will: The Three Wills of God, R.C. Sproul talks about the three different wills of God. The first will is the decretive will of God or the sovereign will of God. This is God's ultimate will which is only known to Him, and He carries it out when and how He feels. An example of this was the creation of the earth. He spoke it, and it came into being. He created it all in six days and then chose to rest on the seventh day. This will cannot be stopped and fits into the larger picture of God's story for us human beings.

The second will of God is the preceptive will of God. "The preceptive will of God relates to the revealed commandments of God's published law. When God commands us not to steal, this "decree" does not carry with it the immediate necessity of consequence. Where the light couldn't refuse to shine in creation, we can refuse to obey this command. In a word, we steal" [xxviii]. Put more straightforward, it is up to us, who have free will, to decide whether or not we follow God's will.

The last type of will is the permissive will of God. "What is usually meant by Divine permission is that God simply lets it happen. That is, He does not directly intervene to prevent its happening" [xxix]. We see examples of this throughout the Bible; when God allows Joseph's brothers to betray him (Genesis 37:28), when He allows Saul to hunt down David (1 Samuel 24:2), and He allows Pharaoh's heart to remain stubborn to Moses and Aaron's request (Exodus 7), to name a few. The permissive will is the type of will that God allows to happen to get us closer to fulfilling his decretive/providential will.

It's important to note that the preceptive will cannot occur outside God's decretive will. God will never ask you to do something that doesn't align with his decretive will. They all fit together like a puzzle in our lives. Sometimes we can see what God is doing, and other times we have to obey what he tells us to do without knowing the outcome. Like Abraham, who took a step of faith to leave his home and go to a new land without knowing where he was going. God knew one day that Canaan would be the Promised Land of his descendants. Abraham needed to trust God that whatever His will was, it was good and pleasing and perfect. He knew that God knew best.

The word for will in Romans 12:2 is the permissive will of God. God reveals His will to us, but it is up to us to follow it. Subsequently, this is the same Greek word used for will in Luke 22:42: "Yet I want your will to be done, not mine." This Scripture shows us two things: firstly, we were created with free will. God created us to be loved and to love Him; He created us for a relationship with Him. The second thing the Scripture shows us is that we have a choice. We get to choose if we follow God's permissive will for our lives or not. Of course, as Christians, we want to follow God's will for our lives because, just like Abraham, we know that He knows best. His ways are higher than our ways, and His thoughts are higher than our thoughts (Isaiah 55:9). It's our job to trust God as we obey Him, trusting that His will is good, pleasing and perfect for our lives.

DENYING YOUR FLESH

> *Our difficulty is not that we don't know God's will. Our discomfort comes from the fact that we do know His will, but we don't want to do it.* - Henry Blackaby

This quote is an excellent example of how we should view the will of God. The problem isn't that we don't know and therefore can't do His will, but that we do know and don't want to do it. Can you imagine if Jesus decided not to die on a cross? Just take a moment and think about where you would be? What would your life look like? I don't know about you, but I'm forever grateful for everything the Cross represents in my life. Was it hard? Yes! Was it worth it? Of course, it was, and Jesus would do it again and again if he needed to.

Let's look at those last moments before Jesus was arrested and ultimately crucified. Jesus had just finished eating the Passover meal with his disciples (The Last Supper) when He decided to go to the garden of Gethsemane and pray with a few of them. Matthew 26:37-39 states,

> He took Peter and Zebedee's two sons, James and John, and became anguished and distressed. He told them, "My soul is crushed with grief to the point of death. Stay here and keep watch with me." He went on a little

farther and bowed with his face to the ground, praying, "My Father! If it is possible, let this cup of suffering be taken away from me. Yet, I want your will to be done, not mine (NLT).

God spoke directly to him, and He knew what was to come and how gruesome it would be. He knew death was imminent; that's why he was "anguished and distressed," and his "soul [was] crushed to the point of death." (tense changed). The Greek word for anguish or sorrow is *lupeo*, which means deep emotional pain, severe sorrow [xxx]. The Greek word for distressed is *ademoneo*, which means to feel fear, lack courage, or be troubled [xxxi]. Lastly, the Greek word for crushed or very sorrowful is *perilupos* which means engulfed in sorrow [xxxii]. All these words paint a bleak picture of how Jesus was feeling the hours leading up to His death. However, He still maintains, "Yet, I want your will to be done, not mine." Simply, He trusted God. He trusted that God's will was best. He trusted that God would take care of Him. Although He died, He rose again. He trusted God.

I think it's essential to look at what was happening physically with Jesus during this process leading up to this death. After all, He was human. Luke 22:44 says, "he was in such agony of spirit that his sweat fell to the ground like great drops of blood." So on top of feeling all those intense emotions, He was sweating blood. I'm no medical expert, but to truly get the complete picture of what was happening with Jesus, we should look at what was actually happening to him physically. The medical term is *hermatohidrosis*. It is "a condition in which capillary blood vessels that feed the sweat glands rupture, causing them to exude blood, occurring under conditions of extreme physical or emotional stress." [xxxiii].

We also have to consider that Jesus being human, was probably going through the physical response of fight-or-flight. "The fight-or-flight response (also known as the acute stress response), refers to a physiological reaction that occurs when we are in the presence of something that is mentally or physically terrifying" [xxxiv]. Your body goes through a chain reaction where the sympathetic nervous system is activated, stimulating the adrenal glands that release catecholamines (adrenaline). This, in turn, increases your heart rate, blood pressure, and breathing rate. You may also experience dilated pupils, pale or flushed skin and trembling. So, on top of intense negative emotions and sweating blood, He had to deal with all the physical reactions from the fight-or-flight.

Jesus had to deny his flesh. He had to deny every physical side effect He felt that was stopping Him from what was to come. As we see above, it's natural for our bodies to literally protect ourselves when in trouble. However, in the midst of all of that, Jesus still chose to trust. He knew He had to remain obedient to God, even to the point of death. Jesus was the ultimate living sacrifice. God may not be calling us to obey Him to the point of death, but He does call us to go against the grain. As we saw in Romans 12, God doesn't want us to "copy the behaviour and customs of this world." He wants us to follow His will, to ensure that His will is fulfilled in our lives. For Jesus, that took self-control and an extreme focus, and of course, He had His Heavenly Father helping Him through this traumatic event. We are blessed today to have the Holy Spirit as our help. The Holy Spirit is there on the inside of us, cheering us on when it's tough, reminding us what we need to do, convicting and empowering us to do the right thing. What is God asking you to lay aside so that you can fulfill His will in your life?

Denying your flesh may not look like Jesus' story. But what's your story? What is God asking you to lay aside so that you can fulfill His will in your life? Could it be pride? Greed? Anger? Hate? Unforgiveness? The Bible clarifies what happens when we *don't* deny our flesh.

Galatians 5:19-21 states,

> It is obvious what kind of life develops out of trying to get your own way all the time: repetitive, loveless, cheap sex; a stinking accumulation of mental and emotional garbage; frenzied and joyless grabs for happiness; trinket gods; magic-show religion; paranoid loneliness; cutthroat competition; all-consuming-yet-never-satisfied wants; a brutal temper; an impotence to love or be loved; divided homes and divided lives; small-minded and lopsided pursuits; the vicious habit of depersonalizing everyone into a rival; uncontrolled and uncontrollable addictions; ugly parodies of community. I could go on (MSG).

It's clear what happens when we give in to our flesh. Do you see yourself in any of those traits? If you do, like I have many times, seek God to change your heart and help you deny your flesh.

CHOOSING TO DO THE RIGHT THING

We are constantly faced with the decision as human beings, especially as Christians, to do the right thing. The Bible says in Romans 12:1: "And so, dear brothers and sisters, I plead with you to give your bodies to God because of all he has done for you. Let them be a living and holy sacrifice—the kind he will find acceptable. This is truly the way to worship him" (NLT). We are meant to be a living sacrifice. Have you ever stopped and think what that actually means?

A sacrifice is defined as "an act of giving up something especially for the sake of someone or something else" [xxxv]. Matthew 16:24-25 says, "If any of you wants to be my follower, you must give up your own way, take up your cross, and follow me. If you try to hang on to your life, you will lose it. But if you give up your life for my sake, you will save it" (NLT). Essentially, Jesus calls us to sacrifice our lives for Him at the Cross as He did for us. This is a choice we must make daily. For us to give up our lives like that requires trust. We need to trust that God will provide for us and help us do what we need to do that day. We also need to trust God that He has our best interest at heart and wants what is best for us.

God's preceptive will is that we lay our lives down every day to take up our cross. We have to choose every moment of every day to do the right thing. It's not an easy feat, and we have the help of the Holy Spirit to do it. I am faced with the decision every day when I get into my car to drive. I'm a driver who can be a bit aggressive. I like to get to my destination on time, so I'm usually on a mission. Unfortunately, other drivers do not share my sentiments— especially the sweet old Sunday drivers. You know the ones I am talking about; they take their good ol' precious time on the road. Going the exact speed limit, if not a little under it. I have learned that instead of tailing them, it is better to take my sweet ol' time as well. I'm embarrassed to say that there have been times that they have saved me from getting a speeding ticket.

This is what a living sacrifice looks like practically- choosing to do right when everyone around you is not.

A friend told me that it's better to be an offensive driver than a defensive driver. Offensive drivers see the dangers and proactively avoid them. These drivers are not selfish. They look out for patterns of how other drivers drive around them and anticipate their needs over their own driving needs. I have to admit, that was a foreign concept as I saw driving as a way to get from point A to point B. However, I know with my mind that it's better to be an offensive driver who allows drivers to cut in line, cut me off, come in front of me, etc. There would most likely be fewer accidents if we were all offensive drivers. This is what a living sacrifice looks like practically- choosing to do right when everyone around you is not.

Elijah also chose to do the right thing in the face of opposition. In 1 Kings 18, we read that Elijah was just confronted by King Ahab - King of Israel, along with 450 prophets of the false god, Baal, on Mount Carmel (1 Kings 18:19). At this point, Elijah realizes that he is the only prophet of God left (1 Kings 18:22). Elijah, who has had enough of the idol worship, challenges them to a contest of power to prove that God is real. God obviously wins this contest for Elijah and demonstrates His power (1 Kings 18:38). In the very next chapter, we see Elijah fleeing because Jezebel, King Ahab's wife, threatens his life. He runs to the wilderness, where God finds him under a tree. 1 Kings 19:9 says, "But the Lord said to him, "What are you doing here Elijah?"" God never sent him to the wilderness. Elijah was running away from his problems.

Next, we see God show Elijah who He truly is. 1 Kings 19: 11-12,

> "Go out and stand before me on the mountain," the Lord told him. And as Elijah stood there, the Lord passed by, and a mighty windstorm hit the mountain. It was such a terrible blast that the rocks were torn loose, but the Lord was not in the wind. After the wind there was an earthquake, but the Lord was not in the earthquake. And after the earthquake there was a fire, but the Lord was not in the fire. And after the fire there was the sound of a gentle whisper (NLT).

Shortly after that, God asks Elijah to go back and appoint another king over Israel and Aram. He immediately obeys God and does the right thing by going back.

God wants us to be a living sacrifice so that He can use our lives to fulfill His will. He wants to use our lives to further his kingdom. If we aim always to do the right thing, He can move through our lives. On the flip side, we have to remember that God is ready to correct us if we mess up, but not in a loud oppressing voice, but a gentle whisper. I believe God does this because He wants to speak to our hearts. During the times when God gently whispers to our hearts, intimacy with our Creator is formed. This allows us to trust Him more, enabling us to sacrifice our lives for Him daily. See the pattern? We grow in intimacy with Him, we trust Him, and, in turn, we lay our life down for Him.

Dietrich Bonhoeffer says it well, "Being a Christian is less about cautiously avoiding sin than about courageously and actively doing God's will." God's will for us is to do the right thing; by obeying His Word. He wants us to choose to take our daily cross, be the living sacrifice that constantly says yes when the rest of the world is doing the complete opposite. It looks like laying down in front of God, remaining open and vulnerable with God, and allowing Him to use us for His will. Yes, it's trust at its finest; trust when it's most difficult.

WHEN YES IS THE ONLY OPTION

I have also been there. I can say with confidence that if you are reading this book right now, it's because you have been through trials in your life, your faith has been tested, and you have struggled to trust God throughout it all. As mentioned before, God took me through a season of testing, shaping and moulding shortly after receiving the "promised" position. Instead of using my circumstances to help me pass the tests and grow, I allowed them to push me down; I felt the weight. However, throughout this whole season, God never gave up on me. He was always there, guiding me and speaking words of life over me.

There was a moment during this season, as I mentioned before, I had lost my car, our church had just opened up a new campus (first time ever), and I was living on my own. It was the first time I truly felt alone - at home and at work. Of course, that wasn't actually the case. I had friends who were willing to do Costco runs for me, take me grocery shopping, drive me to church and lend me their vehicles to run errands. But I couldn't rely on that. During this time, I wanted to quit so badly.

There is a Bible Study by Havilah Cunnington called I Do Hard Things. It's about learning to do the hard things in your life while breaking off shame and fear (Check out the resources section for this Bible study). What I remember most about this time is how many new things I had to do. I had to outfit four kids' classrooms from scratch without a car to transport items to and from each campus, to create new checklists, processes, and procedures for this campus while running a supply drive. It was a lot all at once. I felt the pressure.

It was natural that I wanted to give up, but something inside me stopped me from actually doing it. One day God whispered in my heart, "Remain faithful." The following day during my devotional, He gave me Luke 16:11: "When you are faithful with little, you will be faithful with much." Basically, He was saying that if I remained faithful to my job, then one day, He would promote me. Let me be clear that I did not remain faithful in the hopes of promotion but to be obedient to God. Promotion comes from Him, and as much as He spoke about promotion, it didn't mean that it came in the way I expected it to or like I thought.

> Happy are those who remain faithful under trials, because when they succeed in passing such a test, they will receive as their reward the life which God has promised to those who love him (James 1:12, GNT).

God does not intend for us to go through trials to feel the weight but to gain new strength.

Remaining faithful when we are going through trials requires trusting God. Remember the definition from chapter one; trust is choosing to lie down on the ground before someone. In this case, it's taking the trial to God, and saying, "Here you go, God. I know you have my best interest at heart. Give me strength to pass this test." It's giving our pressure, weight and burdens over to God. Matthew 11:28-30 says,

> Come to me, all of you who are weary and carry heavy burdens, and I will give you rest. Take my yoke upon you. Let me teach you, because I am humble and gentle at heart, and you will find rest for your souls. For my yoke is easy to bear, and the burden I give you is light (NLT).

We are not designed to carry the weight of any season alone. God does not intend for us to go through trials to feel the weight but to gain new strength. He wants us to succeed and overcome. As we trust God with our problems, He will give us the rest we need in that season.

Jonah was another person who was facing the burden of a call. When God called him to announce His judgment against Nineveh, he ran in the opposite direction (Jonah 1:1-2). In his defiance, Jonah ends up getting on a boat going in the opposite direction. While on the ship, they encounter a violent storm. The seamen throw lots to see whose sin brought on the storm. They end up finding out that it was Jonah. Jonah offers to be thrown into the sea. He gets swallowed up by a whale and remains there for three days. He prays to God, and God orders the whale to spit him back out. Then God calls Jonah, again, to go to Nineveh and proclaim His judgment against them. Jonah finally obeys.

That was a wild story, but I'm sure God used drastic measures to get Jonah's attention. After all, Jonah deliberately disobeyed God, and he needed to deliver the message to Nineveh. Picture this: Jonah in the belly of the whale after he deliberately disobeyed God. He probably thought, "This is it; I'm done for. This is where I'm going to die. This is my punishment for disobeying God." However, that wasn't his response at all. He had time to think in the belly of the whale, and this was part of his prayer, "But I will offer sacrifices to you with songs of praise, and I will fulfill all my vows. For my salvation comes from the Lord alone" (Jonah 2:9, NLT).

This was a prayer from someone who completely trusted in God. Although he ran, at first, he knew what needed to be done. That's why when God saved his life and called him,

It's better to

trust

God with the unknown in your life rather than take matters into your own hands.

"Yes!" was his only option. Knowing that God has your best interest at heart, and knows what is best for you, is trust. Jonah trusted God that there was a reason He was asking him to proclaim His judgement over the Assyrians. All He wanted him to do was obey. Is there an area of your life that you are avoiding saying "yes" in? I want to encourage you that your Yes to God will always be better than your "no". Sure, it takes trust, but may I also suggest that it's better to trust God with the unknown in your life than take matters into your own hands.

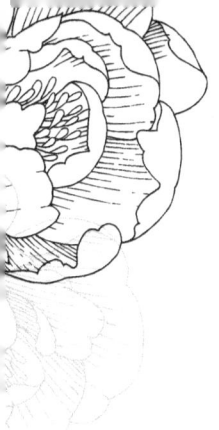

Journal about what God is asking you to give up in order to follow him?

JOURNAL

DOODLE IT!

Draw/Doodle the timeline of your testimony.

QUESTION

Do you know what God's will is for your life? Are you following or pursuing it?

CHAPTER 9

Trusting God's Will

GOD'S ACTUAL WILL FOR OUR LIVES

> *It is good to remind ourselves that the will of God comes from the heart of God and that we need not be afraid.* - Anonymous

What is God's actual will for our lives? I believe it can be found in Matthew 28:19-20:

> Now wherever you go, make disciples of all nations baptizing them in the name of Father, the Son and the Holy Spirit. And teach them to faithfully follow all the I have commanded you. And never forget that I am with you every day, even to the completion of this age (TPT).

This Scripture can be summed up in one phrase; "help people find and follow Jesus" [xxxvi]. God's will is that we tell people about Jesus wherever we go and teach them how to follow Him once they say yes. That's how we make more disciples, the Great Commission.

This command can be challenging to digest if this doesn't come naturally to you. However, if we look at the last part of the Scripture, it says to "never forget that I am with you every day." We don't need to try and fulfill God's will in our own strength. In fact, Jesus promises that He will be with us "even to the completion of this age." He promises to always be with us. I don't know about you, but just knowing Jesus is with me all the time already strengthens me. He also left this earth so that we could have the Holy Spirit living on the inside of us. This Spirit empowers us to do things out of our comfort zone.

I wouldn't be here today if someone were not following God's will for their lives.

My church's mission is: "Helping people find and follow Jesus." This is God's Preceptive will for all Christians as a whole. Like that of the Ten Commandments, we choose whether or not we want to follow God's will. I wouldn't be here today if someone were not following God's will for their lives.

Romans 10:14-15 says,

> But how can people call on him for help if they've not yet believed? And how can they believe in one they've not yet heard of? And how can they hear the message of life if there is no one there to proclaim it? And how can the message be proclaimed if messengers have yet to be sent? (TPT)

It is why God needs us, and He tells us plainly in His Word what we are to do. It ties in with salvation. Jesus saved us so that we can help others get saved. We can't make disciples if we haven't become a disciple ourselves and said yes to Jesus in our own lives.

Getting out of our comfort zone requires *trusting* God.

What does that look like in our lives? For everyone, it is going to be different. Some excel in going up to strangers and talking about their personal life, and some can easily approach someone and begin to pray with them. Some can meet others' practical needs, and someone else is good at having people in their home and welcoming them. Yet others are good at teaching those who have already come to the faith.

Wherever you are on that spectrum, it's going to take trusting in God to fulfill His will. We need to lay down our lives; be a living sacrifice to how we are typically dispositioned. Getting out of our comfort zone requires trusting God. When we do things that are not natural to us, we trust God that He will be with us and give us the wisdom and strength to succeed. When He asks us to go up to someone and say hi or smile, and/or ask if they need help, we can boldly do this, trusting that we are empowered to do the task.

One of the best ways to share Jesus with others is to tell your story. Before I knew Christ, I was a very private person. I did not share personal details about my life with anyone, and I kept a wall up because I didn't trust people. And then someone helped me find Jesus, and God has shown me how powerful my story is.

In the fall of 2019, I got the chance to film my testimony at a local Christian TV station professionally. I knew it would take time to edit it and air, so I waited. In the meantime, God asked me to film my testimony on my own and post it on social media. I was scared, and I didn't want to do it. I avoided doing it and disobeyed God because I was scared to be that vulnerable with everyone. Months later, I bit the bullet and filmed myself. Two days after I posted my video, the Christian TV station finally posted my professionally filmed testimony on social media without letting me know beforehand. The video was delayed in being aired due to COVID lockdowns. I was so frustrated with myself because I had just posted my amateur filmed testimony merely days ago. If I had only obeyed God earlier, my professionally filmed testimony would have been an add-on to what I was supposed to share earlier.

I had to trust God when both times I sat down to film my testimony. I did both because of my willingness to lay down my life on the ground in front of God. I am so grateful He could use me. I was able to encourage and inspire bravery in others. All because I said yes to God and decided to trust Him. I was able to help people find Jesus by sharing my story of finding Jesus (For more on my testimony, head to the back of this book).

WHAT'S IN YOUR HAND?

Now that we know God's actual will for us as believers, how do we begin to figure out what that looks like in our lives? Sure, like I mentioned before, telling your story is a great place to start. But let's go deeper.

I have always loved the story in the Bible when God shows Moses what He can do. In Exodus 3, God tells Moses that He is sending Him to lead His people out of Egypt. Moses questions God, and legitimately concerned about the enormous task ahead of him, asks a fundamental question twice, "What if they won't believe me or listen to me? What if they say 'The LORD never appeared to you'" (Exodus 4:1)?

Let's pause right there. Can I just say how much I love that Moses asks this question? These are real concerns and fears that he has. God isn't just sending him to talk to His people, but convince them to believe in a God that, probably most have doubted due to their years in slavery, is actually alive and wants to save them. It takes trust to be able to do something like that. Especially since Moses grew up in the palace while his people suffered in Egypt. No wonder he thought they wouldn't listen to him.

We know he ended up going and doing it, but why? Let's go back to our Bible story. The moment Moses questions God, God answers him back with a question, "What is that in your hand" (Exodus 4:2)? Moses was holding a shepherd's stick at the time. God gave him instructions for the staff, and Moses watched God perform miracle after miracle using this ordinary everyday item. He encouraged Moses to show the Israelites these miracles so that they would believe that God spoke to him.

At that moment, I believe God was showing Moses that He had already equipped him for the task He sent him to do. The very thing in his hand was what God was going to use to fulfill His will in Moses' and his people's lives. Moses had a choice; trust that God actually equipped him and step out to do the task God asked him to do, or not trust God. Because he chose to trust, he eventually led the people out of slavery and Egypt.

This got me thinking about my own life. Many times, as a result of reading this passage, I would ask God, what's in my hand? What do you want me to do? I remember the first time I asked God that question; I held a pen in my hand. I now know what God wants me to do, but back then, I was oblivious. God is not a God of confusion; He is a God of clarity and wants to show you what He has planned for you to do.

I chose to also trust God as Moses did, and as a result, by the time this book comes out, I will have started writing my third book. This illustration seems simple, but I want to encourage you that it is that simple. It took me a while to get here, and it may take you a bit as well. Remember that God is in control and wants you to do what He created you for. Trust Him with this and watch Him show up.

I didn't always know what God wanted me to do with my life. I felt stuck at times while I pursued other things besides writing. That's another thing that I need to note. God could be waiting on you to get out and start doing something, anything. How will you figure out what God wants you to do when you aren't even trying to do something?

Start literally with what's in your hand. What do you find you pick up the most throughout the day? A broom? Maybe cleaning is your thing? A guitar? Maybe God wants you to write songs? A baby? Maybe God wants you to create something that will make motherhood easier?

A cup of tea? Perhaps you will be the next tea sommelier? You get it, find something and start doing it. If it's not for you, then move on to something else. You will get it.

In the meantime, learn to trust God in this area of your life. After all, it is His will that we want to see manifested in our lives. The same will that He created us in our mother's wombs to fulfill here on this earth (Psalm 139:16). Sure, it may look different than you expected, but when you learn to trust Him, He will always show up.

EVERYONE PLAYS A PART

> *You won't fully enjoy a swing unless you raise your feet from the ground. You won't fully enjoy a boat unless you remove the rope's knot from the riverbank. Never limit yourself when it comes to trusting God.* - Anonymous

How is it that we can believe in the impossible for others but not for ourselves? This quote tells us that we can't place God in a box when it comes to trusting Him in our lives, and we can't expect Him to do the impossible for others and not expect Him to do the same for us. God has a purpose for all of us and a specific plan for us to fulfill that purpose.

1 Corinthians 12:12-14 says,

> There is one body, but it has many parts. But all its many parts make up one body. It is the same with Christ. We were all baptized by one Holy Spirit. And so, we are formed into one body. It didn't matter whether we were Jews or Gentiles, slaves or free people. We were all given the same Spirit to drink. So the body is not made up of just one part. It has many parts (NLT).

You have a role to play in the Great Commission. You are part of a larger picture to God. It's not up to you to ensure the salvation of every person you meet. Your job is to do that one thing, which is God's specific will for your life. To do this, it takes trust. Trust that God will be with you every step of the way as you step out to obey what He tells you to do. If you don't know what God wants you to do, ask Him. Be specific because He wants you to be doing that thing. Just remember that He may not give you the whole picture, but He definitely wants to provide you with the next step.

Let me state clearly, that you are not defined by who others are or what they do. You are only defined by who God says you are and what He calls you to do.

I want to talk to those struggling with where they fit within God's larger will for every

Christian. As I mentioned before, I wrestled with this for years. I allowed comparison to force me into spaces I was never meant to be. I tried to be something I was not and went places God never asked me to go. I thought I was doing the right thing because others around me were doing it. I thought I was fulfilling God's will for my life. But all I was really doing was allowing comparison to tell me what I wasn't and trying to measure up to that. Let me state clearly, that you are not defined by who others are or what they do. You are only defined by who God says you are and what He calls you to do.

It is important to note that God's timing is perfect. We talked about this before; we can't rush or slow down God's perfect timing. It took me some time to begin reaching out to people in my walk with God. I brought a lot of baggage into my relationship with Jesus, as all of us do, and it needed to be removed. I needed to work through it, and I needed to heal. That took time. It was a process, and I had to trust that God's timing was perfect.

I now know that God wants me to write; however, my writing journey wasn't seamless. I always liked to write, whether it was chronicling my life in my diary or writing poetry. Writing was a way to process my feelings as a deep feeler. I remember receiving my first diary when I was ten years old. It was pink and purple, and it had a gold lock on it with a key. As much as I loved it, I didn't really start using it until I was a teenager. I was going through so many changes in my body that I felt comfortable writing about all those emotions rather than talking about them. I then started to write poetry to express those deep feelings. I even won a contest with one of my poems. I really like writing, but then I stopped doing it when I went to university.

When I said yes to Jesus in my late 20's, I still wasn't writing. Fast-forward three years later, and the Holy Spirit tells me that I would write my first book on purity. I laughed. I had never written a book. The most I had written was my Masters' thesis at university. But I obeyed, and the result was that I ended up publishing my first book four years later. After I wrote it, I still didn't see how it fit into the Great Commission. Yes, I was telling people about Jesus, but I was having more of those one-on-one conversations about how Jesus transformed my life.

It took another two years to finally start sharing the heart behind my book and my testimony. You see, my book is just another way that I was getting my life story out there. I realized that sharing my story and how Jesus changed my life and what I learned from that was what God was calling me to do - that was the part that God wanted me to play.

John 4:37-38 says, "You know the saying, 'One plants and another harvests.' And it's true. I sent you to harvest where you didn't plant; others had already done the work, and now you will get to gather the harvest." (NLT). You have a part to play, and you are exactly where you need to be right now to fulfill it. You are on the right track. Even in my moments where I felt off track, I was where I needed to be to lead me to this moment now.

Remember, Jesus said that the harvest is great, but the workers are few (Matthew 9:37). I feel like we can count ourselves out of the race because we don't know what to do. It's essential to do something and start somewhere. I know that it will lead to the thing that God has for you - the one thing that gets you excited about the Great Commission.

Trusting God is essential to us fulfilling His will in our lives.

Purpose and calling are very personal things to us. And if you aren't fulfilling yours, it can be a sensitive topic. Yes, God calls us to trust Him even in this most vulnerable part of our lives. I mean, why else did God call us? To continue living life the same way we had always lived it?

No, He wanted us to live our lives on purpose - God's purpose. Trusting God is essential to us fulfilling His will in our lives. Trust allows us to get out of our own way and enables God to move us in the direction of His will.

It was a journey, and it didn't happen right away. So if you are feeling lost and not sure where you fit in, remember that God has a place for you. He has something specific that fits within His bigger will for your life. He has a unique way for you to help people find and follow Jesus. So be patient. Learn to trust in His timing; it will be worth it.

JOURNAL

Journal about where you see yourself in Moses' story of being called by God to set the Israelites free?

DOODLE IT!

Draw/doodle what you want your life to look like- no boundaries or restrictions. Just DREAM!

QUES
TION

Where do you see yourself in the bigger will of God for the Great Commission?

CHAPTER 10

God's Timing is Perfect

THERE IS ALWAYS AN APPOINTED TIME

God has an appointed time for everything under the sun. He has set aside each event to happen at a precise moment (Ecclesiastes 3:1). This can become less hazy to see when you have been waiting a while for your promise to come.

As I mentioned in a previous chapter, I have been waiting for a promise of a spouse for multiple years. For some of you, you may have been waiting much longer than me, and for others, not as much. At the end of the day, we are all waiting for the same thing together. Waiting can be challenging, and it can really weigh you down.

I'm going to come right out and say it. Waiting has been hard! I was placed in charge of weddings in my church. I had asked for years to be over this ministry, and they finally gave it to me a couple of years ago. God's timing is perfect. At this time in my life, I struggled to hold onto my own promise of marriage. I'd waited so long and had so many failed experiences in this area of my life that I was through with waiting. The Bible says we weep with those who weep and celebrate with those who celebrate (Romans 12:15).

With each wedding I coordinated, I was

The length of my *wait* does not determine the fulfilment of my promise.

celebrating in my heart of hearts. But deep down, I longed for a spouse of my own, a wedding that I could plan and get excited about. I had well-intentioned friends and colleagues who encouraged me, telling me that my day would come. However, I saw my promise slipping through my fingers as time went by. It became hard to hold onto it. I wanted to give up, and as I mentioned before, there were moments I did.

Something that has brought me comfort recently is knowing that there is actually an appointed time for what I am waiting for. Habakkuk 2:3 states, "It aches for the coming - it can hardly wait! It doesn't lie. If it seems slow in coming, wait. It's on its way. It will come right on time." This verse speaks of God's appointed time for the vision. It's not that the promise will never happen. God promised it, and He has His own timing of when it is going to happen - "it will come right on time."

The promise doesn't change just because you have to wait for it. I had to learn this hard truth. The length of my wait does not determine the fulfilment of my promise. I realize that I need to be careful the longer I wait. We have an enemy out there, and he is walking around like a roaring lion, looking for someone to devour (1 Peter 5:8). He would love nothing more than for us to give up on our dreams and lose hope in our promise. But we have to remember that giving up cannot be an option because our blessing is coming (Galatians 6:9).

I have to lay down what I don't see around me to embrace the faith that God has given me.

Having faith that there is an appointed time for my marriage, a spouse, and one day kids takes a lot of trust in God. I truly believe that God gives the most faith to those He tests the most. I have clung to this Scripture over the years: "We live by faith and not by sight" (2 Corinthians 5:7, NIV). I have been told numerous times throughout my single journey that I just need to focus on what God is doing in my life because one day, I will look up and notice that someone else is running alongside me. Well, I just want to say that when I look up from the work I am doing now and then, I don't see anyone running with me. I have no other choice than to choose faith. I have to lay down what I don't see around me to embrace the faith that God has given me. Faith to believe in a promise that seems so far-fetched.

Being yielded to God lays down our thoughts and predispositions and takes up God's ways of thinking.

The Greek word for faith in 2 Corinthians 5:7 is *pistis*. It means "belief, trust and confidence" [xxxvii]. HELPS word studies state, "Faith is always a gift from God, and never something that can be produced by people. In short, *pistis* for the believer is "God's divine persuasion..." The Lord continuously births faith in the yielded believer so they can know what He prefers" [xxxviii]. We need to trust God to grow in our faith. Being yielded to God lays down our thoughts and predispositions and takes up God's ways of thinking. It requires a laying down, which requires vulnerability. In essence, this is trust. Our faith grows as we learn to walk with God and embrace His ways.

I am learning to exercise my faith step by step by choosing to trust God in this area of my life. Some days, it's easy, and other days it's not as easy. All God asks is for us to trust Him; He can take care of the rest.

So maybe you are like me, and you are waiting on a spouse, or perhaps for you, it's a ministry opportunity, a new job, or a baby. Whatever it is you are waiting on, remember that God wants to give you the faith to trust Him during this season. He has an appointed time for your promise, and He doesn't want to give it to you prematurely, but right on time.

IT'S WORTH THE WAIT

As a single Christian today, I have had these

words uttered to me on several occasions: "It's worth the wait." They were talking to me about waiting on my spouse. I can write about this now and not cringe, but it wasn't always like that. There was a time when hearing those words would push me into a tailspin of emotions and thoughts. I would think, 'how is the wait worth it when the object of my wait seems so far away from me?' The wait was hard at that time. How could all this longing and suffering be worth it in the end? I tried to see a way forward, but my sight failed me. I was in a place of disappointment and discouragement; my heart was heavy.

"Hope deferred makes the heart sick, but a dream fulfilled is a tree of life" (Proverbs 13:12, NLT). My heart was sick. I couldn't grapple with the fact that God was saying to me, "not yet." The thought made me sick to my stomach. Why not? I would think. Why isn't it my turn yet? I couldn't understand why God had me waiting so long. I had failed attempts at meeting guys and people around me getting engaged or married. Sound familiar? Well, I was in this place of despair for 18 months. It became dark all around me; the cloud hung over my head wherever I went.

The Hebrew word for sick in Proverbs 13:12 is *chalah*, which means to be rubbed down or worn, to be weak, sick, afflicted or to grieve, make sick" [xxxix]. Benson Commentary says this about the first part of this verse: "The delay of that which a man eagerly desires and expects is such an affliction, that it differs little from a lingering disease" [xxxx]. That means when the waiting gets long, Solomon (who wrote the Book of Proverbs), in all his wisdom from God, knew that it could feel like a lingering disease that won't go away.

But the story doesn't end there. God doesn't want us to feel afflicted to leave us in this place. He wants to give us a way out. So, where do we get our cure for this disease? Let's look for our answer in the book of the prophet, Isaiah: "He was pierced because of our rebellions and crushed because of our crimes. He bore the punishment that made us whole; by his wounds we are healed" (Isaiah 53:3, CEB). If anyone knew about afflictions, it was Jesus. Jesus experienced beating, lashings, being spit on, insults and mockery and one of the most physically exhausting trips to Golgotha. He waited eight days to make His journey from being arrested to being crucified and finally dying and rising again.

What spurred Him on? His eye was on the prize. He placed His hope firmly in God, knowing the reward that lay ahead of Him. He trusted God that what He said would happen would actually happen. He didn't look around Him but focused on God. Hebrews 12:1-2 states,

> There, since we are surrounded by such a huge crowd of witnesses to the life of faith, let us strip off every weight that slows us down, especially the sin that so easily trips us up. And let us run with endurance the race God has set before us. We do this by keeping our eyes on Jesus, the champion who initiates and perfects our faith. Because of the joy awaiting him, he endured the cross, disregarding its shame. Now he is seated in the place of honour beside God's throne (NLT).

Because Jesus endured the cross, we can endure our own crosses.

We run the race set before us; however, it looks. For me, part of my race is waiting on the promise of God for a spouse. For you, it may be something else. I know that the only way we can do this is by keeping our eyes on Jesus. Like I talked about in Chapter 7, looking up places us in a posture of vulnerability, a posture of trust. Because Jesus endured the cross, we can endure our own crosses. He trusted that God was going to turn His sacrifice into our blessing. And God did. The last sentence says that He now sits in a place of honour beside God in heaven.

God wants you to win in life. He wants you to be able to experience the blessing on the other side of your race, on the other side of your wait. At the end of it all, Jesus wasn't cursing God. It said that Jesus yelled and then released his spirit (Matthew 27:50). It looks like He just gave up, but He gave in. In this small moment, Jesus relinquished control over his body and trusted in God. Let's just imagine for the sake of this book that at this moment, Jesus' body whispered, "It's worth the wait." And because of His obedience, He now wears a crown.

This admittedly gives me hope and a new perspective on the words "It's worth the wait." We see what happened to Jesus, and I can look around and see others on the other side of their wait.

Yes, they are happy, and no, it's not perfect. But having gone through the waiting season, the end result is worth waiting for. I can't wait to say that one day when I'm on the other side of my wait. But in the meantime, I fix my eyes on Jesus, knowing my promise of marriage will be fulfilled and my wait will come to an end.

Our present troubles will be but a distant memory in the fulfillment of our promise.

God wants to give us beauty for ashes (Isaiah 61:3). He wants us to accept that it is worth the wait. Our present troubles will be but a distant memory in the fulfillment of our promise.

The second part of Proverbs 13:12 states, "a dream fulfilled is a tree of life." Benson Commentary says, "That is, most sweet, satisfactory, and reviving to the soul" [xxxxi]. It is what God has for us on the other side of our wait. Will you trust Him with the timing? Will you trust Him with your affliction? Will you trust Him with your current pain? If you do, God promises a revival of your soul. Now that's something to look forward to.

SURRENDER TO HIS TIMELINE

> *Be careful about rushing God's timing. You never know who or what he is protecting you or saving you from. - Reverend Lucy Natasha*

We have already learned that God has a time for everything, an appointed time when everything will happen. So why do we get impatient? Why is it hard for us to accept God's timing when something will happen in our lives? For me, I struggle with not being in control. I am a Type A personality, I like things a certain way, and I want to plan for every possible outcome. Couple that with a person who likes to plan my future for fun! So when I'm asked to wait for an outcome and timeline that is unknown to me, I squirm. Patience is one of the fruits that the Holy Spirit is still working within me. It's not in my nature to be patient.

I was born a twin. I have a twin brother. Before

you ask, yes, it was great having a brother as a best friend growing up, but I still wish I had a sister. He is thirteen minutes older than me, which he loves to rub in my face whenever he gets a chance. After he was born, I waited a whole thirteen minutes before I came out of the womb. The only time I probably was glad to wait in my life as I had my mother's womb all to myself. I jest, but I always think back to my baby self and wonder what I was waiting for because that is so uncharacteristic of me today.

To thrive in these times of waiting, I realize that I need to learn to surrender to God's timeline and let go of mine.

I was the little girl who was involved in everything. I played soccer, tee-ball, ballet, jazz, tap. I modelled and participated in pageants before the world of Toddlers and Tiaras was even a thing. As I got older, I stopped all of that to pick up piano, the recorder and karate. I was always the girl on the move. I like to go, go, go, and I'm not very different today in my late 30's. To thrive in these times of waiting, I realize that I need to learn to surrender to God's timeline and let go of mine.

It's hard for me not to plan and go with the flow. I remembered a few years ago when I went on my third missions trip. We supported some missionaries in Cambodia, and our church decided to make our first trip out there to see their work. So keep in mind this was the first time our church had sent people out there. We were meant to go on this trip a year earlier; however, we had to cancel it due to the political unrest happening in the country. Six of us signed up to go the second time around, and two pastors came along. We had a rough plan for what we would do out there, and my heart was happy. After going on that trip, I can confidently say that no day went to plan. Every morning during our trip, we would meet with our pastors, and they would run through the plan for the day. It changed every day, from day to day, and even from moment to moment.

For someone to go against their nature and submit to an unknown timeline requires trusting the One in control.

God was indeed creating a spirit of flexibility and surrender in me with this trip. I couldn't hold onto the plan given to us in paper form anymore. I had to go with the flow; I had to surrender to God's timeline and what He was doing through our trip. That takes trust. For someone to go against their nature and submit to an unknown timeline requires trusting the One in control. God was in control. At that moment, I chose to trust God. I decided to lay down my agenda and wait each day for the daily bread He had for us.

During this trip, we got the chance to minister to their worship team, inspire their dance team, minister to kids living in all sorts of living conditions, pray over struggling people, minister to their pastors and spread the love of Jesus. We had an adventure or two on the tuk-tuks (the local mode of transport. You should try it sometime if you are ever in Cambodia), and try some outstanding Asian cuisine. By far, it was the BEST trip I had ever been on. Although I have gone back again, nothing can replace what God did in me during that trip. And all it took was me to sit back and trust God.

"Be still and know that I am God" (Psalm 46:10, NLT)! The word for still in this passage in Hebrew is *raphah* which means to sink, relax, abandon and let it go [xxxxii]. There needs to be confidence that we know who we are waiting on for us to be still. God's Word says, "and know that I AM God." (Emphasis added). We see these words "I am" at the beginning of Exodus when God calls Moses to lead his people out of Egypt. After God finishes telling him what he must do, Moses asks Him who he should tell the Israelites He is. God responds, saying, "I AM WHO I AM. Say this to the people of Israel: I AM has sent me to you" (Exodus 3:14, NLT). Knowing the great I AM is having intimate knowledge of who God is and His power.

Knowing the great I AM is having intimate knowledge of who God is and His power. We don't trust our circumstances because they can change as they did on my missions trip. However, we focus on the great I AM who has our best interest at heart. Like David says in Psalm 46, we are still because we know God. We know that when He is in control, He is working it all out for our good. We can relax and sink and let our situation go knowing that God's timeline is the best timeline for our lives.

BEFORE IT'S TIME

> *Stress makes you believe that everything has to happen right now. Faith reassures you that everything will happen in God's timing.* - Marcus Lamb

With God's appointed timing, we can't do anything to make it happen quicker or slow it down. God already appointed the time it will happen in our lives long before our lives took shape (Psalm 139:16). However, we can try to make something happen with our own effort and strength. That's where we can get into trouble.

We saw that Abraham and Sarah tried to make

the promise happen in their own strength, and he had Ishmael. Ishmael wasn't the promise (Genesis 16). The Israelites impatiently created their own God to worship in the form of a golden calf statue while waiting for Moses to come back down from the mountain with instructions from God (Exodus 32).

For somebody like me, that's something that I have struggled with over the years—learning to wait on God's perfect timing and not going ahead of Him for the sake of getting things done. I am a natural doer. When things need to get done, I do them. I plan and execute. When I do that, I strive to make things happen in my life outside of God's timing. The end result is that I usually fail, or it doesn't go well.

There was another family in The Bible who had to wait for Jesus. In the eleventh chapter of John, we meet Martha and Mary, Lazarus' siblings. They were good friends with Jesus and knew Him well. Lazarus was sick (John 11:2). One day Mary and Martha sent word to Jesus that their brother was sick. "Although Jesus loved Martha, Mary and Lazarus, He stayed where He was for the next two days." (v.5-6). He finally decided to go back and see them. By the time He reached, Lazarus had died.

It's important to note what He said as soon as He heard about Lazarus being sick. "Lazarus' sickness will not end in death. No, it happened for the glory of God so that the Son of God will receive glory from this" (v.4). What made Jesus so confident that Lazarus' sickness wouldn't end in death? Just ten verses later, Jesus finally tells His disciples that Lazarus is actually dead (v.14). So why would He contradict Himself? Jesus knew God and trusted His plans. He knew that Lazarus would have to die to be resurrected. He also knew that his death would not be in vain.

The story ends with Jesus finally arriving in Judea and calling out Lazarus from his grave. Lazarus, bound in graveclothes, comes out with his face and head wrapped up. Jesus asks them to remove those from him and let him go. He lives (v. 43-44)!

Jesus knew that his Father in heaven had perfect timing for everything to happen. If He had gone as soon as He got the news, then He wouldn't have been able to perform His third resurrection miracle. Remember, He said that it would be for God's glory. I wonder how many people came to believe in Jesus that day and at that moment? Verses 15-16 say, "And for your sakes, I'm glad I wasn't there, for now you will really believe. Come, let's go see him." Thomas, nicknamed the Twin or doubting Thomas, said to his fellow disciples, "Let's go, too - and die with Jesus."

There are a couple of things we can glean from these verses. Firstly, Jesus explains why He didn't go sooner and why He needed to wait. He knew the miracle of resurrection was coming, and He knew that this moment would change believers' and unbelievers' hearts for good. It could help us too if we knew why we were waiting. However, sometimes we don't know why God wants us to wait. He just wants us to obey. But if we learn anything from Jesus in this Bible story, it's essential to not go before God's timing. God has a plan and needs us to trust Him and be obedient to where He calls us and what He calls us to do.

Secondly, by Jesus waiting, he knew it would help Thomas' and other disciples' doubt. The same Thomas who doubted if Jesus was real when he saw Him after resurrecting from the dead. (Side note: I think it's interesting that it took a resurrection for Thomas to believe both times. Just saying.) It's impossible to doubt that Jesus is who He says He is when He performs a big miracle like resurrecting someone from the dead. The disciples were willing to go with Him even though they were risking their lives to have a front-row seat to what Jesus was about to do. Jesus did deliver. God was glorified.

Verse 25 says, "Then Jesus wept." I want to make it clear that Jesus struggled with his decision. He loved Lazarus very much, so it must have been hard to hear he was sick and then find out he died. It must have been one of the hardest things for Him to wait on God's timing. That takes intimate trust in the Father. It requires laying down His own emotions and thoughts in front of God and allowing God to have all the control.

Sometimes the wait can be painful, but the results are always worth it.

If you are struggling to trust God with his timing and are tempted to take matters into your own hands, remember this story of Lazarus. Remember that God is working all things together for your good (Romans 8:28). Sometimes the wait can be painful, but the results are always worth it. Let's be a people who wait on God's perfect timing with the confidence of what is to come.

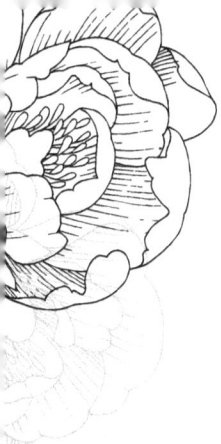

Journal what this quote means to you: "the promise doesn't change because you have to wait for it."

JOURNAL

What does it look like to be still and know God? Draw/doodle it.

DOODLE IT!

QUESTION

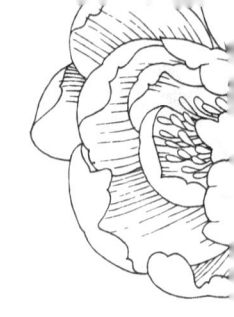

How have you felt having to wait for your promise in this season of wait?

_____
_____
_____
_____
_____
_____
_____
_____
_____
_____
_____
_____

CHAPTER 11

God Always Comes Through

WAIT, WAIT, WAIT

If you're anything like me, being told to wait after you have already been waiting a while is not good news. But when God is involved and asks you to wait longer, you must remember that He is creating something special for you. So be expectant. The Bible says that "no eye has seen, no ear has heard, and no mind has imagined what God has prepared for those who love him" (1 Corinthians 2:9). We can't begin to fathom what God has in store for us. He is creating something new for us that we have never seen or imagined. So yes, when I say to be expectant while we wait, it's because something good is coming our way.

Romans 12:12 in the Message version encourages us to "be cheerfully expectant" in our times of waiting. The Greek word for expectant is *elpis* which means joyful and confident expectation [xxxxiii]. We should know that what God has promised will come to pass in our lives. Like I said earlier, that can be hard when you have been waiting a long time.

Last year, I saw God come through incredibly in my life. I just finished giving my notice to move out because my friend and I decided to move in together. It was also in the middle of the first COVID-19 lockdown our city went through (later, we would come to have three more), so we weren't sure what would happen.

A month in, not many places were up for rent because of the lockdown. We had seen many places, but each place we went to didn't suit our needs. We had made a list of things we were looking for in our new apartment; two fairly even-sized rooms, a living room, outdoor space, good storage, and a decent-sized kitchen that would allow both of us to be in at once. All of this in a beautiful, walkable downtown borough and within budget.

On top of all that, I had my own list; I wanted a newly renovated place with big windows and lots of light. My current apartment had been newly renovated before I moved in; it was gorgeous (remember that one-bedroom apartment that was at the high end of my budget?). I knew I wanted the same, but I was willing to compromise. We were coming to the end of the second month of my notice, and I had to ask my landlord for an extension because we still had not found a place. Fortunately, she found finding a tenant to replace me was challenging, so my landlord agreed to give me another month's extension.

By this time, more apartments were coming on the market. We were looking at apartments a few evenings a week. I felt like Goldie Locks; one had no living room, another was too small, one didn't have a good layout, and another had absolutely no parking. I have to mention that both my roommate and I had cars we needed for our jobs, so parking was essential.

We finally found an apartment that was a bit smaller than we wanted, but it was renovated two years prior, so it looked good. The only hiccup was that it reeked of smoke. The previous tenant smoked, and as someone who has suffered from asthma in the past, I just couldn't live there. There was permit parking on the street, and it was in that walkable beautiful downtown neighbourhood we were looking for. It was sad, but then the real estate agent mentioned another apartment they were renovating that would be available for our move-in date. Get this, it was around the corner from the smoky apartment we had just seen.

We walked up the stairs and through the front porch door, walked down the hall, and opened up the door to the apartment. It was definitely being renovated; drywall dust was everywhere. Beneath the dust, there were two floors, an outside patio, a large bay window in the living room, granite countertops and two decent-sized bedrooms, one on each floor. Did I mention that there were all new stainless-steel appliances, including a dishwasher? There was also a smaller room across the bedroom, a built-in washer and dryer and tons of storage. This place was perfect. The only thing was that it was way out of our budget. We had to let it go and keep looking. After looking for a couple more weeks, I suggested that we counter-offer for a lower rent amount.

The landlord agreed, and we got the place! We signed the tenancy agreement two weeks before we were supposed to move out. There was no extension this time around; I had to move out. That season of waiting was stressful. But I'm so glad I waited on God. On top of blessing us with a fantastic apartment, He put us in the middle of some great neighbours. I could have never imagined that I would be living in a place like this. I wanted a newly renovated apartment, and this is precisely what it is, and it has two floors. That means my roommate and I can have our own space. I'm currently writing in our office as she learns how to play the guitar downstairs.

> *If you think God has forgotten you, then you have forgotten who God is.* - Anonymous

Waiting for my new place was not easy, but I chose to trust God through it all. I decided to lay all my fears down before Him and embrace His hope that He had something good in store for me, even though I didn't know what it was. This place is such a blessing to us in more ways than one. All because I chose to trust God, trust Him to provide for me. There was a resolve in me to wait on God until I saw His promise manifested in my life.

Someone once told me they had a vision about me of a dog with a bone that doesn't want to let go. That person said that I was tenacious like that dog and that when things get hard, I choose not to give up, but I hold on. And that's what I want to encourage you with today. Have you been waiting on something that you're not sure how it's going to turn out? God has not forgotten you because you are still waiting. Lay it before God; I dare you. Choose to trust Him with the object of your wait. And watch Him turn your waiting into a blessing.

STANDING STILL AND KNOWING

There was a woman in the Bible who was a great example of trusting God. Her name was Esther. She was a Jewish orphan who was raised by her cousin Mordecai (Esther 2:7). As someone who had lost her whole family at a young age, she was probably eager to have a family of her own. King Xerxes (King of Persia) sent a decree throughout the land looking for a new wife after he dissolved his marriage to Queen Vashti. The only prerequisite was that she had to be beautiful.

Mordecai then convinced Esther to go to the palace and start preparing to see the King. The

Bible says that she impressed Hegai (the King's eunuch) and was treated specially, given seven maids to help her and moved into the harem's best place (Esther 2:9).

She then underwent twelve months of treatments just to go before the King. First, she waits her whole life to meet a spouse and then she was advised by her cousin to be presented to the King, to then wait another year before she can even go before King Xerxes for him to maybe choose her or maybe not (Esther 2:12). I'm sure that waiting in this season would have been hard for her.

In the meantime, she did get all sorts of beauty treatments, and she got a whole new wardrobe she was able to choose from to make herself presentable. I can see the entire Pretty Woman montage with the actual song Pretty Woman playing as she gets to try on new outfits and receives elite beauty treatments that only royalty experienced [xxxxiv].

Esther was finally chosen to be Queen. Soon after Esther became Queen, Mordecai found out what Haman was planning against the Israelites. Haman had a personal vendetta against Mordecai and decided to plot to destroy the Israelites. Haman convinced King Xerxes that the Israelites living in Persia at the time were a threat to his kingdom as they were continuing to grow in number. So, he suggested that they be killed (Esther 3:9).

However, God had a plan. While being chosen to be King Xerxes' next wife, God would use Esther to deliver her people. Mordecai approached Esther and convinced her to take an audience with the King. Royalty customs at the time specified that no one could approach the king without being invited (Esther 4:11). Although Esther was deeply disturbed by the news of her people being destroyed, she wanted to respect the customs. Mordecai finally convinces her by saying this:

> "If you keep quiet at a time like this, deliverance and relief for the Jews will arise from some other place, but you and your relatives will die. Who knows if perhaps you were queen for such a time as this?" Esther 4:14 (NLT)

After a time of prayer and fasting with her eunuchs, she boldly came before the King and asked him to save her people on that fated day.

It's important to note the Persian culture at the time of King Xerxes. The reality of this time was that men treated women as objects. Women were not chosen because of their character or intellect but because they were beautiful. Queen Vashti was banished because she refused to dance and sing to please the King. Esther was uprooted from her family to be primped, polished and beautified and paraded in front of the King. The only reason King Xerxes chose Esther was that her beauty pleased him. Although this is important to know, I want to focus on her season of waiting to be Queen for the purposes of this book, and how her obedience in trusting God led her to deliver her people. What she chose to do in the waiting is what interests me.

Esther had to stand in the truth that she was made Queen "for such a time as this". God was working out the salvation of her people in a way they didn't see coming. Esther needed to stand in what she knew; she needed to know who the God she served was. She needed to stand and know.

Let me clarify that standing is not passive; it takes guts and strength.

Let me clarify that standing is not passive; it takes guts and strength. For Esther, it looked like praying and fasting for three days and three nights (Esther 2:16). It meant seeking God and his Word in what she was about to do. It meant seeking God's heart for what she was asked to do. It meant going to the source for her help, direction, and the right words to say to the King.

I can relate to the story of Queen Esther, especially what I went through as a little girl. I had to overcome a lot to stand in the truth of who I was and who I was created to be. I have had the privilege of seeing God use my life in many ways, which I know about and which I may never know about. One of those ways is being able to share my story with you.

> *Trusting God does not mean believing he will do what you want, but rather believing he will do everything he knows is good.* - Ken Sande

Have you ever heard the saying, "God knows best!" Well, He does. At the beginning of this chapter, I talked about how no one has seen or heard the things God has prepared for us (1 Corinthians 2:9). God has good things for us. Sometimes good can look different to us, but He works all things together for our good (Romans 8:28). All He asks is for us to stand and know- He asks us to trust Him. Will you?

PROMISE KEEPER

God's promises are essential; that's why there are so many of them. There are 8,810 promises in the Bible. 7,487 of those are promises God made to humankind. The actual word "promise" appears in the Bible 100 times. The Hebrew language in which the Old Testament is written does not have a word for promise in its language. Instead, in this Testament, we find words like "word, speak, and say" used. Basically, God's word itself is the same as a promise.

Similarly, the dictionary definition of a promise is "to make a declaration assuring that something will or will not be done" [xxxxv]. That's what God does. His promises are declarations that He will do certain things in our lives. We can count on them and lean on them in times of hardship.

In 2013, God spoke a word to me very clearly that I would have a happy and wonderful marriage and that He predestined a mate for me. Fast-forward eight years, and I am still waiting on that promise. I have the words written down, and over the years, I stopped looking at them and then literally put them on a shelf. At the beginning of this year, God asked me, "Can you believe in me to bring your husband this year?" My first response was, of course, I know you can God. And then, my second response was, "God, I struggle to believe this; help me with my unbelief."

You see, last year, God spoke some words over me regarding this area of my life, and they did not come to pass. I didn't struggle to believe that God could actually do it, but He would do it in a specific timeframe. Then God challenged me at the beginning of this year, and I knew it was time to get those promises over my future marriage off the shelf. So I wrote them out again on another piece of paper with the date on it, and for 40 days and 40 nights, I prayed and declared those promises over my life.

A few things happened to me during this time:

1. My faith was stirred for this area of my life like never before. It started to seem possible again because we know that God is the God of the impossible. Nothing is too hard for him.
2. I felt encouraged in this area of my life for the first time in years.
3. I felt strengthened spiritually, emotionally and mentally to continue waiting.

Knowing that I have something specific, an actual promise from God to wait on gave me hope for this area of my life.

Knowing that I have something specific, an actual promise from God to wait on gave me hope for this area of my life. I have seen God come through in other areas of my life, time and time again. From providing a new place to live to providing funds for different missions trips worldwide. One thing is clear - God is a promise keeper. That's why Numbers 23:19 says that "God is not a man, that he should lie, or a son of man, that he should change his mind"

(ESV). When God speaks something to us, it will come to pass. 2 Corinthians 1:20 also states, "For all the promises of God in Him are Yes, and in Him Amen, to the glory of God through us" (NKJV). This means that we can count and stand on any promise from God coming to pass.

So why did God make promises to us? Why were there so many of His promises in the Bible to us? Remember the Doubt/Fear Cycle I talked about in Chapter 1? I believe there are three things that God wants to do in the believer when He makes His promise:

1. **He wants to constantly remind us.** Sometimes it can be easy to forget the promises of God in our lives. We need to remind ourselves what they are so that we can continue to stand on them.
2. **He wants to encourage us.** When we have been waiting a long time and become discouraged, His promises are there to encourage us to know that the best is yet to come.
3. **He wants to build us up.** Waiting can be weary, but God wants to strengthen us in the waiting season of our lives. He wants us to be built up by focusing on His promises.

Dwight L. Moody says, "Let a man feed for a month on the promises of God, and he will not talk about how poor he is." So how do we feed on God's promises? By meditating on them. I am currently reading the Bible in chronological order. I highlight each promise I read and put a bright pink sticker tab next to it. Because they are bookmarked, I can go back to each one individually and read them repeatedly. I want to be able, by the end of the year, to look back at my Bible and see all the promises from God that I read.

What is it about feeding on the promises of God that allows a poor man to shift his focus from his natural environment? When we focus on what God can do, everything else around us seems so simple. His focus is shifted from his circumstances and his limited ability to God's unlimited ability, His ability to speak oceans into existence. Trusting in God's promises is accepting His ways are indeed higher than our ways (Isaiah 55:11). It's choosing to focus on the one that can change our circumstances. And that takes actual vulnerability, which is what the Father longs for.

IN THE FACE OF ADVERSITY

The Israelites faced many adversities when it came time to acquiring the Promised Land. They experienced the wilderness for 40 years as they went in circles around the Promised

Land. They faced walled cities, bodies of water and attacks from the current residents. However, Joshua was leading them at the time, and he had a promise from God that "Wherever you set your foot, you will be on land I have given you" (Joshua 1:3, NLT). Therefore, Joshua knew that conquering the Promised Land was going to happen. As they faced enemy after enemy, Joshua had to hold onto God's promise.

Let me set the scene. Joshua and his people just finished witnessing the miracle of the walls of Jericho falling down at their feet as God said it would. Jericho was one of the walled cities they needed to conquer to acquire the Promised Land. They watched how marching around the walls for seven days resulted in victory over that town. Joshua trusted God's promise. With that success under their belt, God led them to the Amorite's land- the town of Ai, to conquer next (Joshua 7:2). Joshua had sent spies to scout the land. Upon return, Joshua commanded 3000 Israelite warriors to go and fight the Amorites, thinking it should be an easy defeat.

The story says that the 3000 warriors ended up being defeated by the Amorites. Joshua couldn't understand why they were defeated, as God led them to conquer the land. The Israelites were even more discouraged by this.

At this moment, Joshua had to learn to trust God even in the face of defeat. It ended up that one of the warriors named Achan had stolen items that were meant to be set aside and dedicated to the Lord during one of their previous raids. As a result, Achan and his whole family were stoned to death, and their bodies burned (Joshua 7:25).

As a leader, that has got to hurt; to see your own people destroyed because of their sin. Even after he told the people over and over to obey God's commands. God had warned Joshua before he set out to "be careful to obey all the instructions Moses gave you. Do not deviate from them, turning either to the right or to the left. Then you will be successful in everything you do. Study this Book of Instruction continually. Meditate on it day and night so you will be sure to obey everything written in it. Only then will you prosper and succeed in all you do" (Joshua 1:7-8, NLT)!

After they killed Achan and his family, they went back to the Land of Ai, ultimately destroying their King and all the people (Joshua 8). So in the face of adversity, Joshua did not give in to his circumstances; he stood on the Word of God. He did not worry about the defeat of his people; he sought God. He did not cower in the presence of defeat; he strengthened his spirit by remembering the promise of God. After successfully defeating the Canaanites, the people renewed their covenant with the Lord. They did this by reading every word in the Book of Instruction in front of the Israelites (Joshua 8: 34-35).

Battles will always need to be fought when going after your promise from God.

There are a few things that we can learn from Joshua when we face adversity in our own lives. God promised Joshua that they would be successful if they were careful to obey His commands. Battles will always need to be fought when going after our promise from God. Will we choose to keep our eyes focused on God or our present circumstances during the battle? There needs to be trust amidst adversity. We need to lay down what we know to be true and hold onto what God says to be true.

When we know God's promises, we can learn to trust God.

It's easy to be scared when we face many enemies all at once. But our confidence should always come from God. In Isaiah 41:10, God promises the people of Israel as they are being attacked from every side; "Don't be afraid, for I am with you. Don't be discouraged, for I am

There is something that happens within the believer when they have a word from God- they become

unstoppable

even in the face of adversity.

your God. I will strengthen you and help you. I will hold you up with my victorious right hand." We can draw confidence that if God is for us, who can be against us (Romans 8:31)? When we know God's promises, we can learn to trust God.

The last thing we can learn from Joshua is that he pressed into the Word of God. As mentioned before, God commanded him to meditate on His Word day and night because that is where his success would come from. As we see him succeed over enemy after enemy, we can conclude that Joshua obeyed God's commands. Psalm 130:5 says, "This is why I wait upon you, expecting your breakthrough, for your Word brings me hope." There is something that happens within the believer when they have a Word from God- they become unstoppable even in the face of adversity.

So, what adversity are you facing today? What enemies do you need to defeat? Remember putting your trust in God allows you to view them from the lens of His promise and power. When you can view adversities in this light, you welcome the opportunity to see God move in your life in miraculous ways.

HE MAKES A WAY

We sing the song at church about God being

the way maker, but what does that mean? What does that even look like in our lives? If we look at the Word of God, we see so many examples where God made a way where there seemed to be no way: parting the Red Sea, parting the Jordan River, the walls of Jericho falling, providing manna and quail in the wilderness, and so many more. Way maker is a characteristic of God; it's who He is.

A man in the Bible who saw God first-hand make a way when there seemed to be no other way was Abraham. As discussed in Chapter 1, we saw God give him a child in his old age of 99. Sometime later, after God provided Abraham and Sarah with an heir, He asked Abraham to sacrifice his son. "Then God said, 'Take your son, your only son, whom you love - Isaac - and go to the region of Moriah. Sacrifice him there as a burnt offering on a mountain that I will show you" (Genesis 22:2, NIVUK). Isaac represented the promise God gave Abraham about having many descendants. He was the answer to his prayers and the blessing to his faithfulness. He wasn't just any boy; he was the son of God's promise.

So, here's Abraham, happy as could be that he received the promise of an heir. Then God asks him to sacrifice his son. Abraham doesn't miss a beat because he sets out on a three-day journey the morning after to go to where God wants him to sacrifice his son. Now, some biblical scholars say that Isaac was between 5-37 years old at this time. The Hebrew word that Abraham uses to describe his son is *naar* which means young lad, boy or youth [xxxxvi]. He would have to be young enough to be tied up and put on the place of sacrifice and not really know what was happening. He also had to be old enough to carry the wood for the burnt offering to the location of sacrifice. For Abraham to go as far as tying up his son, and putting him on the wood, positioning him to be sacrificed, took faith but also took trust. Abraham had to trust in the promises of God. We know from before that Abraham trusted in the character of God. In this instance, he had to trust that God would come through. He had to trust that God wouldn't provide an heir, to just take him away.

The mere thought of sacrificing a fulfilment of the promise went against everything Abraham knew to be true in his life. Through seeing the faithful hand of God in his life, Abraham knew that he needed to lay down everything he had ever known. He had to trust even when others around were confused. I can just imagine what Sarah thought when Abraham took their son on a three-day journey. Isaac questioned why there was no animal for the sacrifice, but Abraham trusted (Genesis 22:7-8). He knew he had to be vulnerable when he struggled to believe that God would do what God said he would do. Abraham had to embrace the truth of God, no matter what it looked like.

The story ends with an angel of the Lord interrupting Abraham from killing Isaac and providing an animal to sacrifice in his place. It turned out that God was actually testing Abraham to see where his level of faith was. Then the angel of the Lord blesses him, confirming that he will make his "descendants as numerous as the stars in the sky and as the sand on the seashore." (Genesis 22:17, NIVUK). What an exercise of faith and nerves. I could just imagine what Abraham was thinking. Yes, he is known as the father of our faith. But to have that faith, there needs to be a deep sense of trust in God that he is the God who will do what He says He will do.

The bridge to the Way maker song goes like this:
> *Even when I don't see it, you're working*
> *Even when I don't feel it, you're working*
> *You never stop, never stop working*
> [xxxxvii]

Can you lay down what you have known previously to embrace God as the Way Maker?

These words beautifully depict what trusting

God looks like: to have confidence that God is always working even though we don't see it and don't feel it. We trust in the unseen to know that God is indeed a way maker. For some, I know this can be a tricky concept. Because of hurt, being let down and trust being broken, learning to trust God can be challenging. God asks us to trust Him in the midst of our pain. He has a proven record of making a way. So, what is one area that God is calling you to trust Him in? Can you lay down what you have known previously to embrace God as the Way Maker?

> *I needed to trust him in order to allow him to truly order my steps and lead me through the process to the promise and purpose that he had established for my life.* - Chrystal Armstrong

You see, trusting God allows Him to take you through the process that leads to your promise. Like Abraham, it's a laying down of all previous knowledge and embracing God's truth. Is it scary? Yes. Is it worth it? Oh yeah! I will be alongside you, taking the same steps of faith to trust God to take me to my promise of a husband. Who will join me?

Journal about a time that God came through when you were waiting on Him? How did that feel?

JOURNAL

QUESTION

What is God asking you to trust Him with? What do you need to lay down before Him?

DO
OD
LE
IT!

Draw/Doodle God making a way in your hard situation.

CONCLUSION

> Trust in the Lord with all your heart,
> And lean not on your own understanding;
> In all your ways acknowledge Him,
> And He shall direct your paths
> (Proverbs 3:5-6, NKJV).

How do we face the question, 'why am I still here?' How do we face our "here" and learn to embrace it while waiting? The answer is simple: trusting God. We have learned that trust requires all of our hearts. As we learned at the beginning of the book, it requires intimacy and vulnerability. Trust is not passive but active. It requires us to act like these verses say in leaning and acknowledging. We have learned that trust is a choice. God doesn't make us trust in Him, but He invites us to trust Him. Like any relationship, He wants us to choose to trust Him. Because when we do, He knows what can happen in our lives.

We know that trust takes vulnerability; it requires emotional nakedness in front of another. In this case, in front of God. Intimacy with God is always good, and we receive blessings for it (Jeremiah 17:8). If we learn to trust God from the depths of our hearts, He knows we would move from disappointment to contentment. Trust is storing up treasures in heaven, knowing that we have a bright future to look forward to as we live righteously. Trust also says I love you, Lord, more than my circumstances, I know who you are, and I can count on that.

Trust keeps our eyes on God and knows that He is working out everything we are going through for our good. Trust knows that He is in the midst of every season and is still moving. When the waiting gets long, trust says that I will not lean on my own understanding of my life. Instead, I will acknowledge Him in this season and be confident that He is in control.

Trust says that I know who God is, and I will stand in that truth over my circumstances. Trust knows the God we serve, and no matter what we face, it says that God is bigger than it. Trust lays down our own timeline to embrace God's. Trust knows God's promise is to always come through. Trust faces fear and doubt and combats it with love.

GOD WANTS YOUR HEART

God's invitation to trust Him is not a blind invitation to follow Him.

God's invitation to trust Him is not a blind invitation to follow Him. No, He has always sought and will continue to pursue a relationship with His creation. He prefers to love us repeatedly until we understand that trust is for our benefit and not His. God desires our hearts so that we can choose to trust, not by force but by conviction.

1 John 4:16 says, "We have come into an intimate experience with God's love, and we trust in the love he has for us. God is love! Those who are living in love are living in God, and God lives through them" (TPT). God longs for our hearts. He knows that giving someone our heart requires trust. Our Father invites us into that trust circle, knowing that He is trustworthy. God seeks to show us how trustworthy He is.

If this is something that you struggle with, I encourage you to ask God, like I did, why He is so trustworthy. He wants to answer your questions; He wants to show you why. Your why will be different than my why. But I hope that this book helped you understand what trusting God can look like and that it is possible. My unique journey was documented in this book, but I'm confident that He will make Himself known to you in a new way. He will show Himself to you as He loves into more profound depths.

TRUST IS THE REMEDY

Hosea was a man who trusted God. In the book of Hosea, God asks Hosea to "go and marry a prostitute, so that some of her children will be conceived in prostitution" (Hosea 1:2a). It is the first we hear of Hosea, so it seems to be his very first prophetic assignment from God. Off the bat, God asks him first to marry a prostitute and, secondly, to be okay with her cheating on him because she's a prostitute, and that's what she does. Can we talk about trust?

I know that this situation is so much more than the above description. Hosea was the first of twelve minor prophets in the Bible. He was a prophet around the same time as Isaiah, and around the time Kings Uzziah, Jotham, Ahaz and Hezekiah ruled over Judah. His ministry spanned 60 years. "More than any other prophet, Hosea linked his message closely with his personal life...Hosea's prophetic word flowed out of the life of his family" [xxxxviii].

God's reasoning behind Hosea's nuptials was this; "This will illustrate how Israel has acted like a prostitute by turning against the LORD and worshipping other gods." (Hosea 1:2b). God wanted to use Hosea's family life as an example to God's defiant people. God then asked Hosea to take it a step further and name his firstborn son Jezreel to symbolize how He would break His people's military power in the valley of Jezreel (Hosea 1:4-5). The firstborn was every parent's pride and possession. For the baby to be a boy is so important to a father. He is a first-time dad, and God asks him to name his child Jezreel. He then asks him to name his second child, Lo-ruhamah, which means "not loved," and his third child, Lo-ammi, which means "not my people" (Hosea 1: 6, 9).

So not only did he marry a prostitute, but when she finally gave birth to an heir, a son, he chose in obedience to provide him with a name that represented God's judgment against his own people. Hosea had to have trusted God to do all that. I can just imagine how he felt. Hosea knew God had called him and waited to be used by Him. Then finally, God instructs him. Yes, he was obedient, but something else inside him allowed him to obey to the point of embarrassment, ridicule, and judgment. He trusted God.

Hosea was able to lay down his own family to be part of his prophetic message. He was able to lay down the names of his children for the sake of his people. He was also able to lay down pride to marry a woman of a questionable reputation for the sake of God's message. Hosea knew what it meant to lay it all down in front of God - he knew what it meant to trust God with his whole life.

Because of his obedience, Hosea's message of redemption for a nation was displayed through his family. God asks Hosea to buy back Gomer, his prostituting wife, and have her live with him again, even though he knew she was unfaithful. It was to "illustrate that the Lord still loved Israel, even though the people have turned to others gods and love to worship them" (Hosea 3:1).

God asks people in the Bible constantly to trust Him with the outrageous. He asked His Son Jesus to trust Him to the cross, Moses to trust Him to flee from the Egyptians, and David to trust Him with his life. I'm sure Hosea had doubts about everything he was asked to do. The moment God asked him to marry a prostitute, I can just imagine him cocking one eyebrow but then choosing to trust God no matter what it looked like.

Where do you find yourself in this story? Is there a situation in your life where you find yourself knee-deep in doubt? Maybe you fear that God will never bring that promise you are waiting on in your life? Do you lack the faith to believe that God will provide that new job you have been waiting for? Do you wonder if God will come through and provide for you?

I am currently not married, and by the time this book gets published, I most likely won't be married. But I choose to trust God more in this area of my life. I prefer to trust in His perfect timing of a future spouse for me. I had to surrender my heart to my own timeline, forgo what I thought to be accurate, stop relying on what I thought should be and take hold of

God's will for my life in this area. At the end of the day, trust is the remedy that I am seeking as I walk out this challenging season of my life. Trust is the remedy to feeling stuck in this season of my life. There is an invitation from a gentle God to come and follow Him, lay down everything before Him, and walk the path He carved out for me long ago. As a result of this journey, I have experienced such peace in the arms of our heavenly Father. My prayer is that you will too.

Trust- Pt 2.

In walked a man
That changed her life.
He was kind
He was considerate
And all he wanted was her heart.
He wanted her,
For nothing in return.
He protected her;
He saved her;
He loved her.
He came into her life;
To create her anew.
A new identity,
She would wear.
No longer used and abused,
But called and beloved.
She resisted,
As she didn't know how to receive.

One day she opened her arms,
And love poured into her life again.
She was whole,
She was restored,
She was redeemed.
Step by step,
She learned to trust.
Trust Him,
Because of who He was
In her life.
Now she grows,
She learns and
She trusts again.

BIBLIOGRAPHY

[i] Bridges, Jerry. "A Quote from Trusting God." Goodreads. Goodreads. Accessed January 26, 2022. https://www.goodreads.com/quotes/733775-trust-is-not-a-passive-state-of-mind-it-is.

[ii] Strong's Hebrew: 982. בָּטַח (Batach) -- to trust. Accessed January 26, 2022. https://biblehub.com/hebrew/982.htm.

[iii] "Was Moses' Name Egyptian? by John Huddlestun." Was Moses' Name Egyptian? Accessed January 26, 2022. https://www.bibleodyssey.org/people/related-articles/was-moses-name-egyptian.

[iv] Dictionary.com LLC. "Self-Esteem Definition & Meaning." Dictionary.com. Dictionary.com. Accessed January 26, https://www.dictionary.com/browse/self-esteem.

[v] Dictionary.com LLC. "Self-Esteem Definition & Meaning." Dictionary.com. Dictionary.com. Accessed January 26, 2022. https://www.dictionary.com/browse/self-esteem.

[vi] "A Quote by Paul Tillich." Goodreads. Goodreads. Accessed January 26, 2022. https://www.goodreads.com/quotes/129557-doubt-isn-t-the-opposite-of-faith-it-is-an-element.

[vii] "Vulnerability." The Free Dictionary. Farlex. Accessed January 26, 2022. https://www.thefreedictionary.com/vulnerability.

[viii] Gaultiere, Bill. "'Fear Not!" 365 Days a Year." Soul Shepherding, March 17, 2020. https://www.soulshepherding.org/fear-not-365-days-a-year/.

[ix] "Rhonda Byrne Quote: 'Faith Is Trusting in the Good. Fear Is Putting Your Trust in the Bad.".'" Quotefancy. Accessed January 27, 2022. https://quotefancy.com/quote/898206/Rhonda-Byrne-Faith-is-trusting-in-the-good-Fear-is-putting-your-trust-in- the-bad.

[x] "Vulnerability." The Free Dictionary. Farlex. Accessed January 26, 2022. https://www.thefreedictionary.com/vulnerability.

[xi] "Trustworthy Definition and Meaning: Collins English Dictionary." Trustworthy definition and meaning | Collins English Dictionary. HarperCollins Publishers Ltd. Accessed January 26, 2022. https://www.collinsdictionary.com/dictionary/english/trustworthy.

[xii] Strong's greek: 4006. πεποίθησις (pepoithésis) -- confidence. Accessed January 26, 2022. https://biblehub.com/greek/4006.htm.

[xiii] "Luke Study #2: Story in a Story." Vox Alliance, June 23, 2018. https://www.voxalliance.ca/devotionals/luke/luke1/luke-study-2-story-in-a-story/.

[xiv] Goodreads. "A Quote by V. Raymond Edman." Goodreads. Goodreads. Accessed January 26, 2022. https://www.goodreads.com/quotes/814981-never-doubt-in-the-dark-what-god-told-you-in.

[xv] Hope, Living. You are Here. 2020.

[xvi] Website, The Official. "Four Types of Love - Official Site." Official Site | CSLewis.com. Harper Collins Publishers, February 13, 2020. https://www.cslewis.com/four-types-of-love/.

[xvii] Website, The Official. "Four Types of Love - Official Site." Official Site | CSLewis.com. Harper Collins Publishers, February 13, 2020. https://www.cslewis.com/four-types-of-love/.

[xviii] Website, The Official. "Four Types of Love - Official Site." Official Site | CSLewis.com. Harper Collins Publishers, February 13, 2020. https://www.cslewis.com/four-types-of-love/.

[xix] Website, The Official. "Four Types of Love - Official Site." Official Site | CSLewis.com. Harper Collins Publishers, February 13, 2020. https://www.cslewis.com/four-types-of-love/.

[xx] Website, The Official. "Four Types of Love - Official Site." Official Site | CSLewis.com. Harper Collins Publishers, February 13, 2020. https://www.cslewis.com/four-types-of-love/.

[xxi] "Mistrust: Meaning & Definition for UK English." Lexico Dictionaries | English. Lexico Dictionaries. Accessed January 26, 2022. https://www.lexico.com/definition/mistrust.

[xxii] "Pursue Definition & Meaning." Dictionary.com. Dictionary.com. Accessed January 26, 2022. https://www.dictionary.com/browse/pursue.

[xxiii] "Attitude Definition & Meaning." Dictionary.com. Dictionary.com. Accessed January 26, 2022. https://www.dictionary.com/browse/attitude.

[xxiv] GotQuestions.org. "When Were Joseph and Mary Considered Married?" GotQuestions.org. GotQuestionsMinistries, February 25, 2007. https://www.gotquestions.org/Joseph-and-Mary.html.

[xxv] The Editors Of Encyclopaedia Britannica. "Sea of Galilee." Encyclopædia Britannica. Encyclopædia Britannica, Accessed January 26, 2022. https://www.britannica.com/place/Sea-of-Galilee.

[xxvi] GotQuestions.org. "Sea of Galilee." GotQuestions.org. GotQuestions Ministries, February 11, 2016. https://www.gotquestions.org/Sea-of-Galilee.html.

[xxvii] "2307.Theléma." Strong's greek: 2307. θέλημα (theléma) -- will. Bible Hub. Accessed January 26, 2022. https://biblehub.com/greek/2307.htm.

[xxviii] Sproul, R.C. "Discerning God's Will: The Three Wills of God." Monergismcom Blog. Monergism by CPR Accessed January 26, 2022. https://www.monergism.com/discerning-god%E2%80%99s-will-three-wills-god.

[xxix] Sproul, R.C. "Discerning God's Will: The Three Wills of God." Monergismcom Blog. Monergism by CPR Accessed January 26, 2022. https://www.monergism.com/discerning-god%E2%80%99s-will-three-wills-god.

[xxx] "4818.Sullupeó." Strong's Greek: 4818. συλλυπέω (sullupeó) -- to be moved to grief with (pass.). Bible Hub. Accessed January 26, 2022. https://biblehub.com/greek/4818.htm.

[xxxi] "G85.Ademoneo." Strong's Greek: 85 ἀδημονέω (ademoneo) - be very heavy, be full of heaviness. Knowing-Jesus.com. Accessed January 26, 2022. https://bible.knowing-jesus.com/strongs/G85.

[xxxii] "4036. Perilupos." Strong's Greek: 4036. περίλυπος (perilupos) -- very sad. BibleHub.com. Accessed January 26, https://biblehub.com/greek/4036.htm.

[xxxiii] Jerajani, H R, Bhagyashri Jaju, M M Phiske, and Nitin Lade. "Hematohidrosis - a Rare Clinical Phenomenon." Indian journal of dermatology. Medknow Publications, July 2009. https://www.ncbi.nlm.nih.gov/pmc/articles/PMC2810702/.

[xxxiv] Cherry, Kendra. "The Fight-or-Flight Response Prepares Your Body to Take Action." Verywell Mind. Verywell Mind, August 18, 2019. https://www.verywellmind.com/what-is-the-fight-or-flight-response-2795194.

[xxxv] "Sacrifice Definition & Meaning." Merriam-Webster. Merriam-Webster. Accessed January 26, 2022. https://www.merriam-webster.com/dictionary/sacrifice.

[xxxvi] Living Hope Church, www.findhope.tv

[xxxvii] 2 corinthians 5:7 for we walk by faith, not by sight. BibleHub.com. Accessed January 26, 2022. https://biblehub.com/2_corinthians/5-7.htm#lexicon.

[xxxviii] "4102. Pistis." Strong's Greek: 4102. πίστις (pistis) -- faith, faithfulness. BibleHub.com. Accessed January 26, 2022. https://biblehub.com/greek/4102.htm.

[xxxix] "2470. Chalah." Strong's Hebrew: 2470. חָלָה (chalah) -- beseech. BibleHub.com. Accessed January 26, 2022. https://biblehub.com/hebrew/2470.htm.

[xxxx] Benson, Joseph. Proverbs 13 benson commentary. BibleHub.com. Accessed January 26, 2022. https://biblehub.com/commentaries/benson/proverbs/13.htm.

[xxxxi] Benson, Joseph. Proverbs 13 benson commentary. BibleHub.com. Accessed January 26, 2022. https://biblehub.com/commentaries/benson/proverbs/13.htm.

[xxxxii] "7503. Raphah." Strong's Hebrew: 7503. רָפָה (raphah) -- sink, relax. BibleHub.com. Accessed January 26, 2022. https://biblehub.com/hebrew/7503.htm.

[xxxxiii] "1680. Elpis." Strong's greek: 1680. ἐλπίς (ELPIS) -- expectation, hope. BibleHub.com. Accessed January 26, 2022. https://biblehub.com/greek/1680.htm.

[xxxxiv] Marshall, Garry, Arnon Milchan, Steven Reuther, J. F. Lawton, Richard Gere, Julia Roberts, Ralph Bellamy, et al. Pretty woman

[xxxxv] "Promise Definition & Meaning." Dictionary.com. Dictionary.com. Accessed January 26, 2022. https://www.dictionary.com/browse/promise.

[xxxxvi] "5288. Naar." Strong's Hebrew: 5288. נַעַר (NAAR) -- a boy, LAD, youth, retainer. BibleHub.com. Accessed January 26, 2022. https://biblehub.com/hebrew/5288.htm.

[xxxxvii] Osinachi Kalu Okoro Egbu, Way Maker, 2016 Integrity Music Europe (admin. by Capital CMG Publishing, Sinach: Way Maker (Live)

[xxxxviii] Swindoll, Chuck. "Hosea." Book of Hosea Overview - Insight for Living Ministries. Insight For Living Ministries. Accessed January 26, 2022. https://www.insight.org/resources/bible/the-minor-prophets/hosea.

RESOURCES

Chapter 2

Books

Relationship Goals
Michael Todd

Outdated: Find Love That Lasts When Dating Has Changed
Jonathan "JP" Pokluda

Websites

The Heart of Dating
https://www.heartofdating.com

Moral Revolution
https://www.moralrevolution.com/singles

Chapter 3

Books

The Four Loves
C.S. Lewis

Forgiving What You Can't Forget
Lysa TerKeurst

Unpacking Forgiveness: Biblical Answers for Complex Questions and Deep Wounds
Chris Brauns

Chapter 7

Book

I Do Hard Things
Havilah Cunnington

Chapter 8

Website

My Testimony on 100 Huntley Street
http://www.100huntley.com/watch?id=230136

ACKNOWLEDGEMENTS

To Justin who proverbially held my hand at the beginning of this process when I was unsure, and for helping me pursue writing again.

To Marisa, who became the second pair of eyes for my book reluctantly, but willingly. I wouldn't be here without you.

To Daria, fellow author, who was there to answer all my questions and encourage me even when I thought I didn't have it in me.

To LaToya who helped me turn my vision into reality while taking me to the finish line!

THANK YOU!

AUTHOR BIO

Amanda Guiseppi is an author of non-fiction, publishing Purify Your Life in 2018. She currently lives in Hamilton, Ontario, Canada, where she works in full-time ministry at her church. Before writing non-fiction, she obtained her Master's degree in Theatre Directing from Royal Holloway University in Surrey, England. Amanda is also an award-winning poet. A Hamilton native, she is a lover of brunch, sleeping in, hiking the many falls within her city, and baking or cooking up a storm in the kitchen. You can visit her online at: *www.amandatheauthor.com*

PREVIOUS TITLE

Purify Your Life takes a look at how to unlock the power of purity in your life. Based on 2 Timothy 2:21; the belief that we can position ourselves to be used by God for every good work as we rid our lives of impurities. This book can be purchased on Amazon.

FIRST READERS *Club*

JOIN US!

Join our exclusive club where readers will get an ALL-ACCESS pass to Amanda the author and all her publications:

- Be the FIRST to get updates on her writing
- Be the FIRST to know when a new book is coming out
- Be FIRST in line to purchase her new book
- Be the FIRST to read her new book, even before it's published!
- Receive exclusive discounts and specials on publications and gifts
- Be the FIRST to participate in GIVEAWAYS and contests!

Join Amanda on her journey through the link on her website today!

ENJOY!

As a THANK YOU for purchasing my book, here is a FREE gift just for you:

1. Open your smartphone camera.
2. Aim at the QR code below.
3. Click on the link that pops up.
4. Enjoy!

www.ingramcontent.com/pod-product-compliance
Lightning Source LLC
Chambersburg PA
CBHW072047110526
44590CB00018B/3069